T0370016

MONEY
MAGIC

A Handbook of
Spells and Charms
for Prosperity

About the Author

Patricia Telesco has been a part of the Neo-Pagan community for over 30 years. During her speaking engagements across the U.S., Trish met many wise people working behind the scenes who blessed her with down-to-earth perspectives for going forward with books and life. Along the way, cooking at festivals led to writing more about culinary topics. The result has been very happy bellies for family and friends alike.

Food is love; food is hospitality. Food changes life, and life changes food.

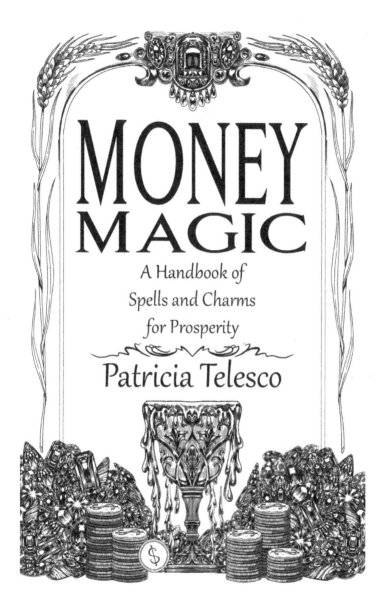

MONEY
MAGIC

A Handbook of
Spells and Charms
for Prosperity

Patricia Telesco

Chicago, Illinois

Paperback ISBN: 978-1-964537-10-8
Library of Congress Control Number on file.

Disclaimer: Crossed Crow Books, LLC does not participate in, endorse, or have any authority or responsibility concerning private business transactions between our authors and the public. Any internet references contained in this work were found to be valid during the time of publication, however, the publisher cannot guarantee that a specific reference will continue to be maintained. This book's material is not intended to diagnose, treat, cure, or prevent any disease, disorder, ailment, or any physical or psychological condition. The author, publisher, and its associates shall not be held liable for the reader's choices when approaching this book's material. The views and opinions expressed within this book are those of the author alone and do not necessarily reflect the views and opinions of the publisher.

Published by:
Crossed Crow Books, LLC
6934 N Glenwood Ave, Suite C
Chicago, IL 60626
www.crossedcrowbooks.com

Printed in the United States of America.
IBI

To those who have not—may you prosper!
To those who need—may you find fulfillment!
To those who struggle—may peace be your companion!
To those who fear—may you learn trust!
Thank you, Spirit, for my readers, friends, and family—this is the best
job in the universe!

Contents

Introduction

"The wealth of man is the number of things he loves and blesses,
which he is loved and blessed by."
—Carlyle Thomas

Money makes the world go around, or so it seems. As much as spiritually centered people might wish for a less materialistic setting in which to nurture the soul, in reality it's almost impossible to get away from the almighty dollar. In fact, greenbacks have a kind of magic all their own. If you don't think so, watch what happens when you waive one under the nose of a picky maître d' at a fancy restaurant who claims to have no seating!

This is just one example of how we are bombarded every day with a flurry of financial fuss, whether it's news from Wall Street, an app with our bank balance, bills, or any number of other monetary matters. I suspect that most folks reading the material shared here don't often go through a twenty-four-hour period without reaching for a wallet, hunting for change in a pocket, or opening a payment app. It is simply the nature of the society in which we live, a sign of the times, and a true testament to the power of the fiscal god and goddess known as Lord MasterCard and Lady Visa!

Unfortunately, the strong presence of these two deities means that many people have bottomed out on the bottom line and overextended themselves. Those of us who are just getting by are getting pretty darn tired of just getting by, and those of us who live on a very tight budget often have to sacrifice desirable spiritual tools and educational materials in favor of buying groceries. All told, there are only so many notches to tighten in that old belt and so many pennies to pinch before someone reaches a breaking point. Then that person says, "to heck with it," splurges, and spends weeks feeling guilty and trying to figure out how to compensate for that binge. The material shared here was written with these realities in mind.

Furthermore, many people I meet in the New Age community have contracted a terrible disease that I call "poverty pox." They somehow equate being spiritual with being poor or of a lower social standing than other folks; some are nearly apologetic for enjoying what they earn through hard work. My response to this is that we are normal, and there's no reason not to reap the benefits of our labors, so a pox on the whole silly idea! It is one thing to choose a meager lifestyle as some type of taboo or an offering to the god/dess, and another altogether to attract that kind of energy into your life. Well, no more! In the information shared here you'll discover a wealth of magical tools and techniques that will help you think profitably, manifest those thoughts prosperously, and enjoy the whole process to boot!

Far more than simply a collection of spells and charms, of which there are many here, *Money Magic* consists of effective self-empowering methods for abundant living every day, no matter your financial situation. Abundance isn't just something that applies to your pocketbook. You can have a plentiful garden, abounding love, bounteous blessings, and so much more, along with a financial flow that will keep those bills paid and maybe even buy a pizza!

More seriously, however, I think a lot of people today feel overwhelmed with financial burdens. Having walked a mile in those shoes, and knowing what a difficult road it can be, inspired the material you'll discover here. My hope is to give everyone reading this a clever, insightful, and practical magical blueprint for changing meager patterns in your life to those that reflect plenty, no matter how you wish to apply that energy. So, join with me now on a whole new adventure in magically grabbing all that life has to offer. You deserve it, and it can begin today!

Chapter One

THE FOLKLORE OF FORTUNES

"The way to wealth is as plain as the way to market. It depends chiefly on two words, industry and frugality; that is, waste neither time nor money."
—Benjamin Franklin

I tend to agree with Mr. Franklin: one of the best ways to ensure personal prosperity is through the magic called hard work and old-fashioned elbow grease. Why? Because Witches and Neo-Pagans acknowledge that they are co-creators with the Divine and the universe. This means that they have to take positive actions to help create the kind of reality for which they wish. It won't be handed to them on the proverbial silver platter. That is simply not the way the path of beauty travels.

Having said that, there is nothing wrong with using magic as a companion to mundane efforts. This energy supports what we're doing in the "real" world. It also provides that all-important inner confidence for the spiritual part of the body-mind-spirit equation to be fulfilled, which is something that we all too often overlook.

A wonderful old Japanese saying states: "One cannot see the whole sky through a bamboo tube." Today, our bamboo tube equates to the family, society, and times in which we've lived. For many people, the diameter of this circle is fairly small, never reaching far beyond the figurative backyard. With this in mind, the information I share broadens some of those horizons and opens that circle to review the charming folklore and superstitions used around the world at various points in history to inspire prosperity.

Why look to folk beliefs, you ask? It is in the superstitions of common people that magical practices often found a safe haven during the times when being a Witch or Pagan was not safe or acceptable. Second, the repeated use of these traditions gives them a tremendous font of energy on which we can draw for spellcraft and ritual. Just consider how much power is generated by hundreds of people repeating the same action, and trusting wholly in that action, throughout hundreds or even thousands of years! That's the kind of energy that folk traditions offer us. Better still, these customs tend to be very simple and pragmatic, making them ideal for the hectic pace of our world.

Using those beliefs and actions as a foundation, the information you find here examines some of the ideas presented to us by great thinkers and seers of the ages with regard to money, prosperity, and providence. There is a lot of wisdom to be found in ancient writings, especially the proverbs. These little tidbits are worthy of thought and meditation, so that our quest for prosperity has a strong foundation of prudence and discernment to guide it for the greatest good.

Folklore and Superstitions

These are really fun to try just because. But as you read through these beliefs, look to the sayings that are familiar to you or the suggestions that have symbols to which you're particularly attracted. Those are the folk traditions that will help you most in your magic because you already feel a connection there. As the electrical outlet supplies a point of contact for energy, your mental or emotional connection with a specific folkway is the contact point for magical power!

- **Agate Offering:** If you place an offering of agates on the altar during the month of June, you will receive financial rewards. Note that if your money situation is particularly adverse, look for black agates with white veins for best results. After you've left the agates on your altar or in a sacred space for a while as a designation of your wish or need, return them to nature so that energy disperses and grows.
- **Alfalfa, Tomato, or Sesame:** Keep alfalfa seeds or sprouts in your home at all times. This inspires providence and prosperity. Alternatively, keep a fresh tomato or a bundle of sesame seeds on your mantle. Note that these last two items must be refreshed as regularly as you want your money refreshed (not to mention the messy, negative association that goes with rotten tomatoes!).

    Because all three of these items are edible, you can also make a great prosperity salad out of them. Blend tomatoes, alfalfa sprouts, and sesame seeds in sesame oil and vinegar dressing and eat expectantly!
- **Almond:** Climbing an almond tree before business deals ensures that a prosperous agreement will be reached. A more practical adaptation of this idea would be eating almonds prior to your meeting or perhaps having them on hand as a snack during the meeting.
- **Aloe:** Egyptian custom dictates that one should place aloe over the doorway of a new residence for success and prosperity. This also acts as a health protector.
- **Animal-Shaped Stone:** In Lapland, Finland, finding a stone that resembles an animal brings the finder luck, health, and wealth.

- **Ash Wood:** Burning this wood in your fireplace or using it as an incense base during the winter months is said to keep everyone in your home from wanting either food or money.
- **Basil:** Place fresh basil in your cash box, wallet, or pocket to attract more customers to your place of business. Salespeople can adopt this idea by keeping basil with important contracts or sales goods.
- **Bell:** Ring a bell whenever you're working prosperity magic. The gentle, bright sound attracts positive spirits who can help you, and it scares away any malicious influences.
- **Bread:** If you'd like to keep the local fairies, who also often bear luck and prosperity in their wings, happy, leave a piece of freshly baked bread on your window. This custom harkens back to old English fairy myths, where leaving a snack for a brownie was an ideal way to pay them back, which in turn provided the landowner with all the help they needed.
- **Camellia Petal:** Floating these petals on water that's flowing toward you will help guide money to your door.
- **Carob:** Early Arabic traders in the Middle Ages used carob seeds to weigh everything—including gold, diamonds, and other expensive goods. This makes it the perfect thing to carry for financial success. What's nice about this is the size makes it a highly portable charm that can be placed in your wallet, where you would wish for more money!
- **Cat's-Eye or Caraway Seed:** Medieval writers say that if you keep a cat's-eye stone with the things you value, it will protect them and attract further opulence. I see no reason not to try this, especially in creating charms and amulets. By the way, if you don't have this stone handy, caraway seeds are a good alternative. These have the secondary benefit of protecting your goods from theft.
- **Cereal:** Eat your morning cereal from the outside of the bowl in toward the center, setting aside a small portion

for the birds. The birds will scatter those "seeds" to the Earth and the winds with your wish so as to manifest ongoing providence in your life.

- **Chamomile or Nettle:** Wash your hands in chamomile tea before handling money or balancing your budget. Chamomile bears vibrations for wealth and success. Alternatively, wash them in nettle water so that money will fall into your palms easily. By the way, both these items can be made into prosperity tea with a little sugar for the "sweet" things in life!

- **Chamomile Incense:** Burning chamomile on your hearth fire attracts prosperity not only for you, but also for everyone in your family or household.

- **Change:** When someone gives you change as a gift, put it into a new purse or wallet. This blesses that item so it will never be empty of cash.

- **Children:** If you want your newborn to always move up in the world, make sure to take them up a set of stairs (preferably in your home) immediately after leaving the hospital. You can also apply this in your own life by making sure to take stairs upward on days you want to improve your standing at work or among a group; take the elevator down so that any disappointments will go more smoothly!

- **Cleaning:** Never sweep dust and dirt out the door; this sweeps away your prosperity. Instead, gather it in the middle of the room first, then transfer it to a dustpan. Additionally, once you're done with sweeping, follow with a damp mop in which fenugreek or fumitory have been added to the water. This attracts abundance.

- **Coal and Jade:** Keep a piece of coal or jade wherever you store your money regularly. The coal helps attract more money; jade improves the financial success that comes from wise business dealings.

- **Coin:** To always have money when you need it, find a coin with a hole through it. Carry this with you everywhere, preferably in your wallet or pocket. On the night of a new moon, spit on the coin and return it to its resting place. This recharges the coin, according to European custom.

- **Coral:** Cultures and societies have used coral as valuable currency in all of human history. Bind a small piece of coral to your wallet or purse. Note that if the coral ever breaks, you should return it to the sea with thankfulness.

- **Corn Dolly:** Put one of these charming decorations in your kitchen close to the stove (but not dangerously so) so that your family will never want.

- **Decoration:** In China, when people wish to bring wealth into the home, they decorate it with images of bats, dragons, or fish. I've adopted two of these customs more literally in my home by owning a bearded dragon lizard and having a tropical fish tank, so the prosperous energy is living.

- **Doorway:** The custom of putting sayings over doorways or on doormats was originally meant as a way of blessing the home. Whatever you choose to put up at the threshold walks into your home with each person that visits!

- **Dowsing for Dollars:** Water Witching was the art of finding wells by the use of a divination rod (a y-shaped branch). There was a similar trick for finding money! In this case, hold a pomegranate branch, sheath of goldenrod, or length of snakeroot in your hand while thinking about treasure. Where the branch, sheath, or root bend down is the place to dig!

  By the way, this is also a good technique for finding valued lost items, so you don't have to spend money to replace them. In this case, however, you would be walking wherever you believe the item was lost, watching for the branch to dip or bob.

- **Emerald:** Carry or wear this stone for riches, health, and happiness.

- **Fennel:** Wearing a crown of fennel improves the power of prosperity magic. However, do not grow this in your garden; buy it instead. Fennel in your garden brings troubles.

- **Fig:** Fig trees are very productive, dropping up to two hundred figs per year, and can maintain their productivity for up to one hundred years. So, if you need to improve things at work and get some recognition, rub the juice on your prevalent tools so a raise will be in your future!

- **Fingernail:** Always cut your fingernails on Friday for the greatest amount of financial success.

- **Fish or Bee Charm:** Victorian people felt that charms bearing the image of a fish or bee were the best types to wear for success in business. Try looking for a carving, a painting, or even a postcard depicting one of these two creatures to keep at the office when you're hoping for a raise!

- **Gem:** There was once a belief in Greece and Rome that some gems had a sex, and if you planted a male one with a female one, they would eventually produce offspring!

- **Hair:** In many ancient traditions, the length of one's hair indicated the amount of prosperity and strength they had; the story of Sampson is an example. In modern settings, this belief can still be found in several Indigenous cultures. And in your life, this might also translate into using hair as a component for abundance and vitality spells.

- **Hazel:** Cap a hazel branch with iron and use it to divine for gold. A modern alternative here would be to follow this custom but use the branch as a wand for casting money spells or for marking the sigils of a sacred circle during prosperity rituals.

- **Honeysuckle:** Put a vase of honeysuckle flowers near a piggy bank, wallet, or any other area where money is stored. This attracts more of the same!

- **Hospitality:** There was a widespread belief in the ancient world that offering hospitality to people would be rewarded with wealth. Mind you, I suspect at least part of that wealth came in the form of new friends!

- **Jade:** Rub a piece of jade before making any important financial decision. This stone will help guide you to success and profit.
- **Kelp:** If you're a businessperson, wash your walkways and doorways with kelp to attract more customers. (Kelp is available in some supermarkets in the guise of alternative sushi wraps.) Alternatively, getting some fresh peas and shelling them on the front porch of your home will have a similar effect. (I personally think this is because people will want to visit in order to snatch a few fresh peas!)
- **Lemon Verbena:** Plant this in your garden so money will grow in your home! Note that this brings a steady flow of income rather than huge surges. Alternatively, plant potatoes and turnips by the waning moon. By the next waxing moon, you should begin to see improvements.
- **Lentil:** Hindu tradition says that lentils draw wealth and continued abundance and are a popular choice when celebrating the New Year. So, the next time you're in need of a little fast cash, make a hearty lentil soup and take the energy of prosperity with you all day long!
- **Leprechaun:** If you capture this mythical creature, hold it tight. Leprechauns so hate captivity that they will reveal the location of great riches to you just to be released. Be forewarned, however, that leprechauns know the art of glamoury and may fool you with an illusion.
- **Lettuce:** When preparing salad, never cut the lettuce, lest you cut off your prosperity. This symbolism came about due to the resemblance of lettuce leaves to dollar bills.
- **Loosestrife:** Plant this near your property. According to various European countries' lore, this protects all your valued possessions from theft.
- **Lucky Penny:** If you see a penny pick it up. As the children's rhyme tells us, this brings good luck. If you

want to use the penny to inspire a better flow of funds, put it in your shoe so prosperity and fortune walk with you, repeating another line of the rhyme:

> *"See a penny, pick it up, all the day you'll have good luck.*
> *Put that penny in your shoe, and good luck*
> *will come to you."*

Or just keep it for pinching!

- **Marriage:** When getting married, one partner should carry three grains of salt and three coins, and the other puts a coin in their shoe. This acts as a charm guaranteeing prosperity.
- **Moon:** In ancient Celtic cultures, a child born under the new moon was believed to be blessed with good prospects and wealth. If you'd like to invoke the new moon's prosperity yourself, here's one simple incantation to recite as you first spy a new moon:

> *"Lady Moon, growing Moon, bring money to me!*
> *Lady Moon, growing Moon, bring prosperity!"*

To improve the results of this spell, bring a silver coin with you and expose both sides to moonlight. Carry it regularly thereafter as a money charm.

- **Moving:** If you're planning a move and can time it for the same day as the when the first sliver of a waxing moon appears in the sky, your home will always have plenty of money.
- **Myrtle:** Greeks, Hebrew, Romans, and the English all regarded this plant as having a prosperous energy combined with good luck. Grow it in your window boxes.
- **Nutmeg:** The Romani people tell us that a way to improve your odds on a lottery ticket or other similar item is to

sprinkle it with nutmeg exactly twenty-four hours before the drawing, race, or other type of timed gambling.

- **Oleander:** Make sure to keep this plant outside your home. Bringing it indoors invokes misfortune.
- **Orange Bergamot:** Rub a bit of this on your money before you spend it so that the cash will return to you (in some form). Carrying this herb also attracts success. The easiest place to get orange bergamot is in the form of tea, which you can also drink before a day of shopping so that your money goes as far as possible.
- **Oven:** Always keep something in your oven, even if it's only an open platter. Empty ovens symbolize want and lack, whereas the platter welcomes providence.
- **Paint Prosperity:** According to feng shui, painting the door to your house red welcomes wealth into the house. If you live in an apartment, try hanging a red cloth on the inside of the door instead.
- **Pomegranate Juice:** An old custom claims that rubbing money with pomegranate juice ensures that the funds will return to you. Because this is messy, I suggest drying a few pomegranate seeds instead and leaving them in the bottom of your change jar to attract more money, literally seeding the jar so money can grow.
- **Ring:** According to some ancient spell books, a tin ring with an amethyst and the symbol of Jupiter upon it brings prosperity. For the most success, however, it should be created on a Thursday during the first or eighth hour of the day.
- **Seeds:** Carrying specific types of seeds attracts money to you. Options include poppy, dock, flax, grains of paradise, and honesty. Alternatively, find a pinch of each and bundle them together in a sachet that you can bear with you whenever you need to hang onto your cash.
- **Silver:** Carry a silver coin minted in the year of your birth into any financial undertaking for the best possible success.

- **Spicy Success:** Victorians and many people during the Middle Ages believed that you didn't need to go any further than your kitchen to find abundance. Spices such as saffron, mint, and cinnamon inspire prosperity, as does eating bananas, oranges, oats, and almonds. If you can blend these items into a rising bread, all the better; the symbolism matches your goal of making your checking account balance rise!

- **Timing is Everything:** The best time to make profitable purchase is when the Moon is in Cancer, Leo, Virgo, Libra, Scorpio, or Sagittarius. Double this power if you can time the transaction for a Thursday, the most propitious day for financial transaction, or a Monday for fortune from business.

- **Turquoise:** Look upon a good quality turquoise right after spying a full moon. Hindu mystics claim this brings immeasurable wealth.

- **Turn it Around:** When you're experiencing a streak of financial bad luck, try using an old gambler's trick to change things. Turn and sit backward on chairs, or turn your socks inside out, to "turn" the bad luck away! I've changed this tradition slightly; I turn over an hourglass instead.

- **Vervain:** Rub yourself with vervain leaves before making a wish for wealth. This helps manifest the wish.

- **Wheat:** If you can gather the last sheaf of wheat from a harvest and keep it safe through the winter, it will bring you luck and providence. Come spring, return it to the land with thankfulness.

- **Wishing Well:** A custom often practiced in Syria instructs that you should go to a nearby well at noon on the twelfth day after Christmas as part of the Christian holiday of Epiphany. If you have enough faith, this water will turn to gold! For non-Christians, this might equate to going to a fountain or handy water sprinkler, then using that water for prosperity potions.

I'm willing to bet that you recognized at least one or two of the aforementioned beliefs as you read them. It's certainly not difficult to see the magic that lies just beneath the surface of folkways. Throughout the material you'll discover here, you'll see where I put many of these ideas to work in spells, rituals, charms, and other magical methods. Remember, however, that these are examples only. Please adapt them so they're more personally meaningful, which will greatly improve the results you get.

Money Omens and Signs

What kind of information did our ancestors leave behind about money omens and signs? What kind of portents tell us that finances are about to dwindle or improve? How can we offset a predicted negative trend, or accent a positive one, through proactive magic?

Here are some of the things to watch for and suggestions as to how to take the greatest advantage of them:

◆ **Ant:** An ant colony taking up residence near your home might be pesky, but it's also an omen of wealth and security. To improve this energy, give the ants a small dollop of honey so they can scatter more sweetness into your life.

◆ **Apple:** When you dunk for apples, be sure to try and bite the biggest one you can. This indicates the size of your financial success in the following year. I'd suggest drying the peel of this apple and using it in prosperity incense.

◆ **Broken Pottery:** If a glass or plate is broken at an engagement party, it indicates that the couple will always have plenty of money. This may have given rise to the custom of breaking a glass after toasting couples good fortune as a way of sealing the magic.

◆ **Cards:** To determine what's happening presently with your finances, get a deck of cards and randomly draw one. If you get a club, you'll make money on a professional endeavor, so enter into it with confidence. An ace of clubs indicates extreme success. The seven of diamonds indicates you'll be making slow but steady progress, and the nine of diamonds or spades reveals the need to tighten your belt as money will be delayed. This last result may indicate that it might be good to wait on any deals or large expenditures for a bit.

By the way, you can adopt this omen into spellcraft and charms by using a club, ace of clubs, or seven of diamonds as a component. For example, you might bless the cards, saying:

"Seven of diamonds, wealth to me bond!
Carried in hand, that's where money lands!"

Keep this in your pocket or wallet and take it out just prior to accepting money in a transaction.

◆ **Cherry Blossom:** In feng shui, cherry blossoms are aligned with prosperity. Add a few to money charms or spells, especially when paired with the color green. Alternatively, add dried cherry blossoms to your money incense blends. And because cherry wood burns longer than most, it makes a great wood-based incense for abundance.

◆ **Cricket and Cat:** If a stray cricket or cat shows up at your threshold, treat it kindly. This is an omen of financial improvements, and the greater kindness you show to the creature, the greater the reward!

◆ **Cuckoo or Lily:** Go to the country on the first day of spring. If you hear a cuckoo calling or find the first lily to open, you'll have a prosperous year. Carry one of the lily leaves or petals with you in the days ahead as a charm to keep the positive energy rolling!

◆ **Daffodil:** Go out in spring and look for the first daffodil to blossom. The Welsh believe that if you find this, you will obtain more gold than silver this year. Mind you that can mean gold-colored clothing, golden beverages, or gold-tone bric-a-brac too! This also means that daffodil petals make a good component for prosperity magic.

- **Dice:** Another way to check the progress of financial matters is to toss a die. If it lands on a six, you can be sure that unexpected money will soon arrive to meet your needs.

- **Egg:** Dreaming of eggs means money will soon be coming your way. The amount is often portended by the number of eggs themselves, such as a dozen indicating $120. Just to support this dream a little more, have eggs for breakfast and internalize that energy!

- **Fern:** Toss a fern frond into the air. If it falls perpendicularly to the ground, that is a good place to dig for buried treasure!

- **Fly:** Finding a fly in a glass from which you were about to drink might be unappetizing, but it is also a sign of forthcoming prosperity.

- **Itching Hand:** If your left hand itches, spit on it and rub it against your pocket. Money will soon arrive.

- **Key:** Keys that rustle for no apparent reason on a Wednesday portend an inheritance. Put this omen to good use! Find an old key and bless it on a Wednesday for financial improvements, then keep it on your keychain as a charm.

- **Ladybug:** If you find a ladybug in your house during the winter season, count the number of spots on its back. This indicates how many dollars or a multiple of that amount you're about to receive.

- **Magpie:** Should a magpie build a nest near your home, it's a very fortunate sign. Put a bay laurel leaf and some breadcrumbs in that tree to honor the bird, look upon it before going on business deals, and you're insured of success!

- **Moving:** If you happen to move to a new house during the waning moon, it's an omen of providence. Should you be unable to schedule the move for that time, keep at least one personal item outside until the waning moon begins (in this case the symbolism is that of troubles waning). At that time, bless the token by the light of that Moon and bring it indoors to keep with your piggy bank or financial papers.

- **New Home:** Watch the physical attributes of the first person to come to your door. According to Scottish tradition, a brunette male or a young boy both portend prosperity soon to follow. You might want to ask a friend over who fits that description!

- **Nuts to You:** Finding a double hazelnut presages wealth and luck. Carry this as a charm or eat it to internalize its positive energy.

- **Oak Gall:** If you find an oak gall and it yields a larva, this portends financial increases. Clean this out thoroughly and keep it near your wallet.

- **Pea:** If you open a pea pod and discover either one or nine peas within, this is an excellent omen for your finances. You can eat these to internalize the energy or dry them to "preserve" your wealth!

- **Ruby:** If you own any piece of jewelry with a ruby in it, watch the stone carefully. If it ever dulls or breaks, be prepared for financial trouble ahead.

- **Sewing:** Thread that wraps around your needle while you sew portends good fortune on the horizon. You can save this piece of thread and use it as a component in other forms of money magic, snip it fine as part of an incense or bury it in your garden so money grows!

- **Shooting Star:** If you can say the word *money* three times when you see a shooting star (before it goes out of sight), it portends prosperity. This would be a nice addition to prosperity rituals and spells during those nights when meteor showers and the like have been predicted by astronomers. Check your local newspaper for this information, which is often located in the weather section.

- ◆ **Spider:** Finding a spider in your clothes speaks of money returning to you, especially funds you considered lost in some manner, such as through poor investments or a stolen wallet. Similarly, a spider in your dwelling is considered a good sign. As the old proverb says, "if you wish to live and thrive, let the spider stay alive!"
- ◆ **Tea Leaf:** Practitioners of *tasseography* (divination by tea) tell us that when bubbles appear in the middle of your cup, it's a sign that money is on its way. To speed things along, I suggest scooping these up in your spoon to gather in the good energy, then drinking the bubbles to internalize that energy!
- ◆ **Thunder:** If you hear thunder in the distance, check the day of the week. If it's Thursday, especially in April or August, you're in luck! Your wealth and goods are about to increase. Keep your eyes and ears open for opportunity's knock!

Now, I know that it's nearly impossible to remember all these omens and apply their instructions on a daily basis. The idea here kind of boils down to recognizing opportunity when it's knocking. All too often, we're moving so fast that we miss a lot of the universe's signals that are trying to guide and direct us to more prosperous and happy living. By learning about omens and signs, you're taking one step toward improving your awareness. As you do, it opens your mind and soul to the quiet voice of Spirit so that life, indeed, will become magical twenty-four hours a day, seven days a week!

A Word to the Wise

Anyone who reads the material I've written knows that I love old sayings, proverbs, and quotes. I have collections that I browse through for the humor, wisdom, and insights they offer. And, because money is something that's been on human minds since the first coins were minted, there's certainly a lot to read!

Let's begin in ancient times. The saying "a man worth his salt" originated in Rome, where the substance was so valuable as to be used to pay soldiers. Adapting this idea, you might want to sprinkle salt around the circumference of your ritual circles. The salt can work double-duty by protecting the sacred space and surrounding you with supportive energy for money magic.

In Greece, a philosopher named Chilon noted that the pursuit of prosperity could be good or ill depending on how people handle themselves on the quest. He said:

> *"Gold is best tested by a whetstone hard,*
> *Which gives a certain proof of purity;*
> *And gold itself acts as the test of men,*
> *By which we know the temper of their minds."*

To my mind, this is great advice that boils down to keeping one's priorities straight! If your family is suffering because you're too focused on cash, you will never have true abundance.

In more recent history, there is a saying: "The secret to making money is saving it." From a magical perspective, this might equate to making a magical piggy bank. Find an unpainted bank to which you can apply sigils of your choosing. Place one special coin in that bank (a seed coin) that will never be removed. Each time the bank gets full, give half the change to a worthy charity and use the rest for a personal need or wish. Return the seed coin to the bank so money continues to grow and return threefold.

Another semi-contemporary man, Benjamin Franklin, said: "If a man empties his purse into his head, no one can take it away from him." This implies that it's a great idea to spend money on your magical education and spiritual focus. It need not be a lot, but a few good books, vinyl records, or CDs and tools make good soul food—and that's the kind of wealth that lasts all eternity!

Two other people, William Austin (author) and John Wesley (preacher), showed us that sharing of our own success and rejoicing in other people's success both create richness of the heart. Austin said: "To rejoice in the prosperity of another is to partake of it." Wesley said the key to financial success is to "gain all you can, save all you can, give all you can."

Finally, we come to Joseph Addison, who promotes the same kind of money magic as I do. He said, "I never knew an early-rising, hardworking, prudent man, careful of his earnings and strictly honest, who complained of hard luck." When we add Mr. Addison's words to those of Benjamin Disraeli, who said, "the secret to success is constancy of purpose," we come up with a powerful formula for success. By being tenacious, truthful, and steadfast, the mundane part of our job will be fulfilled. Add to that a little magic, and what wonders might we achieve?

Chapter Two

PROSPERITY POTIONS AND FINANCIAL FOODS

"...A man hath no better thing under the sun,
than to eat, and to drink, and to be merry."
—The Bible, King James Version, Eccl 8.15

If we truly "are what we eat," why not fill our foods with money magic? Believe it or not, this is something people around the world have been doing for thousands of years. For example, in Japan people eat buckwheat noodles to inspire prosperity on New Year's Day, and in Germany they eat millet! Similarly, Victorian people equated lettuce with money because of its green, leafy nature. So, to maintain prosperity, they never cut the lettuce (this cut off money) but tore it gently instead before they consumed it.

These are the kinds of traditions we'll explore, along with good recipes and sound magical methods for filling both your stomach and your pocketbook! In fact, Kitchen Witchery techniques are among the easiest and most pleasurable ways to make great meals and great magic at the same time.

Better still, because beverages and foods are meant to be consumed, you can slowly savor the flavor of success while literally internalizing the magical energy you've created in your own kitchen. How? By purposefully choosing, mixing, and balancing ingredients known or their positive transformative power and prosperous energies and by using various magical methods while you're preparing them.

Some of the techniques easily added to the cooking process include:

- Prayer
- Incantation
- Visualization
- Blessings
- Charging by the light of the Sun or Moon
- Timing your efforts by astrological correspondences
- Stirring clockwise for positive energy, counterclockwise to banish unwanted energies.
- Lighting a candle of a supportive color while you're cooking (in this case green, gold, yellow, white, and silver are all apt)
- Burning incense that's charged with money-attracting energies (some stores sell money or prosperity incense; otherwise, any aromatic listed here is fine in incense form)
- Serving the food in symbolically colored containers or laying it out in a pattern that symbolizes your goal
- Approaching your kitchen as a sacred space (and perhaps even doing a formal circle casting to stress that magically focused atmosphere)

Don't worry, you need not do *all* these things to get positive outcomes, but at least consider one or two along with the examples I've given here. Additionally, of all these methods, your attitude is the most important one. If you approach anything with respect and reverence, you make it special and sacred. This is certainly true about your proverbial kitchen cauldron.

Some of the traditional components for money, wealth, and abundance include:

- Allspice
- Almond
- Banana
- Barley
- Basil
- Beans
- Berries
- Bran
- Cabbage
- Cashew
- Cinnamon
- Clove
- Dill
- Eggplant
- Ginger
- Grape
- Meat (especially beef)
- Oats
- Orange
- Pea
- Peanuts
- Pear
- Pineapple
- Pomegranate
- Pumpkin
- Rice
- Sesame
- Spinach
- Tomato

I think you can quickly see how even this abbreviated list gives you a lot of options to consider. Bear in mind that you need not have a lot of ingredients for the magic to work effectively. In fact, because you're trying to manifest money, spending it on your components might not be the best approach! A few well-chosen, meaningful items will work just as well in your magic as dozens. For example, a glass of orange juice each day is a good way to internalize both abundance and health! Just get creative and remember to focus on your goals as you create any of these or your own recipes.

Beverages

We consume a lot of beverages. From soda pop to beer to water, each one of those drinks represents an opportunity to internalize a little extra money magic.

Prosperity Punch
The fruits chosen for this beverage are all connected with financial prosperity, but the energy can certainly be internalized with different intentions, such as unlocking a profuse flow of creativity.

- Juice of 1 cup currants
- Juice of 1 cup blackberries
- 1 cup orange juice
- 2 cups apple juice
- Juice of 1 cup cherries
- 1 tbs. honey
- Several grapes (garnish)

Put all the fruit juices in a blender with the honey and whip until the blend is bubbling with energy. Remember to keep your goal in mind while the blender does its part. You might want to add an incantation while the energy is whipping up:

"Abundance of the Earth, give my prosperity birth!"

Drink expectantly and share it with a friend in need!

Strawberry Settlement Frappe
There is nothing more refreshing during the hot summer months than a fruity frappe. Better still, this frappe is designed to help you adjust to difficulties, specifically giving you a better outlook

while financial constraints exist. In turn, this outlook provides a good atmosphere in which to begin manifesting the monetary changes desired.

- 12 cups strawberries, frozen with syrup
- 4 cups ice cubes
- 1 cup berry-flavored syrup (your choice)
- 5 cups sweet cream

Crush the strawberries using a blender or food processor. Follow with the ice cubes, making sure to get about the same texture for both items; this smooths your path and mingles the energies. Mix these two together in a bowl, then return it to the blender in five batches, adding a bit of syrup and 1 cup of cream to each batch. Blend for about five seconds so everything is well mixed. Serve immediately to help you keep a cool head when financial problems are taxing.

Fun Adaptations: You'll find any frozen fruit is wonderful in this recipe. Peaches encourage wisdom so that you use money wisely, cherries help clarify your thoughts about how to make money, and raspberries restore happiness when you're feeling frustrated.

Lucky Windfall Breakfast Juice
In Ancient Greece, pears were associated with the wealthy and the divine, and they're still thought to bestow luck in China and Vietnam. Here we're using that symbolic value to bring a lucky windfall (specifically in the way of cash) our way. Additionally, pears will help you use the money that comes from this spell wisely, spreading it out over a long time.

- 8 oz. pear juice
- ⅛ tsp. almond flavoring

Find a green cup or glass into which to pour the juice. Stir the almond flavoring clockwise into this to generate positive energy as you say:

> *"Spirit of luck, hear my plea,*
> *Through this juice, bring me serendipity;*
> *As within so without, as without so within*
> *By my will this spell begins!"*

Drink to internalize the magic, then go into your day with your eyes and ears open! Don't overlook happenstance moments: That may be opportunity knocking!

Transforming Tea

Make this tea and drink it to shift your aura from one that accepts fate at hand to one that's ready to take on the world and claim your prosperity-*tea*!

- ◆ 2 bags Earl Grey tea
- ◆ 2 cups boiling water
- ◆ 3 raisins (for body, mind, and spirit)
- ◆ Pinch of dried pineapple
- ◆ Pinch of candied orange peel, minced
- ◆ Cinnamon, allspice, and sugar (to personal taste)

For luck, place all your ingredients into the pot before you add the water. Steep for about ten minutes until the aroma is heady. As the water steeps, place your hands palm-down over the pot, visualizing the liquid being filled with vibrant green, gold, and silver light (the colors of money and prosperity). Bless the mixture before drinking it by saying:

> *"Energy and confidence be mine,*
> *Within and without, magic shine!*
> *Negativity bind, abundance be mine!"*

Drink one cup yourself and share the other with a friend in need (remember, good deeds return to you three-fold!).

Charged-Up Coffee

We already use coffee to get our figurative motors going in the morning. This beverage is based on that idea, but adds some energetic, moneymaking herbs to the blend.

- Ground coffee (enough for a full pot in your maker)
- ½ tsp. allspice
- ½ tsp. ginger
- ½ tsp. cinnamon

Mix your coffee grounds with the spices before placing them in the filter. As you put in each spice, you can add an incantation:

> *"With cinnamon, the spell's begun.*
> *With allspice, I claim money and fame.*
> *With ginger so fine, prosperity's mine."*

Perk to literally perk up the energy and give life to your spell!

Fun Adaptation: If you like cream in your coffee, pour about 1 tablespoonful into your cup and swirl it once. Watch what patterns appear to discern how successful your spell was. For example, if the cream moves toward the center of the cup, your luck is soon to change. If it all moves toward the top of the cup (the side away from you), things are looking up! Note that you can use the symbols in a tea leaf reading dictionary to interpret any patterns that appear (or in my book *Futuretelling: A Complete Guide to Divination*).

Feel Terrific Tea Wine

This is one of my favorite wines to enjoy when I'm feeling blue. It requires little in the way of fancy equipment to prepare, it inspires financial improvements, and it always tastes fantastic.

- 12 plain black tea bags
- 1 gallon water
- 1 slice of lemon
- 1 slice of orange
- 2 ½ lbs. sugar
- 2 tbs. sparkling wine yeast

If possible, begin making this just prior to the waxing moon so that the darkness around your life slowly takes on that wonderful silvery glow of positive change! Place the tea bags with the lemon and orange slices in the water and warm. Slowly add the sugar so it dissolves completely. Turn off the heat and let this cool to lukewarm. Meanwhile, suspend the wine yeast in ¼ cup warm water (not hot water, which will kill the yeast). Add this to the tea when the liquid reaches room temperature.

Cover the pot with a heavy cloth for three days. During that time, you'll notice the mix bubbling heartily. Strain the brew through cheesecloth into a glass jug. Cover the bottle top with a balloon to allow for ongoing fermentation. Replace as necessary during the first three months of fermentation.

Strain again, pouring off only the clear liquid; the dark muck at the bottom of the bottle is simply dead yeast. Put an airtight top on the bottle and store in a cold dark place for four to six more weeks. Enjoy as desired. Once you open this, however, you should refrigerate it for a longer shelf life and to preserve the flavor.

Sip this while eating your favorite comfort food and you'll be feeling better in no time. If you don't have time to wait for fermentation, you can use one liter of white zinfandel warmed, in which you steep two tea bags, the orange, and the lemon. Bless this by saying:

"Lift my spirits, with wine so fine;
In me, hope and humor shine."

Fun Adaptations: You can change the flavor of the chosen tea to better suit your needs. If you want to look good for a supportive and financially secure lover, use a blend of jasmine and orange tea. To appeal to a friend for help, use lemon tea; to have the best possible appearance for a job interview, try a blend of ginger and cinnamon.

Success Punch

Prosperity works hand in hand with successful endeavors. When you need to inspire achievement, the abundant blossoms in this brew open the way for similarly bountiful blessings.

- ½ cup woodruff flowers
- ½ cup daisy or jasmine petals
- ½ cup dandelion flower or honeysuckle petals
- 1 quart warm apple juice, wine, or cider
- ¼ – ½ cup heather honey
- 1 orange, sliced
- 1 lemon, sliced
- 1 stick cinnamon

I've offered a variety of flowers here that honor the ancient Goddess, lift a heavy heart, and promote the work at hand. Feel free to mix and match them according to availability to add up to one and a half cups.

Mix the flower petals with the honey and place them in the punch bowl. Slowly pour in the heated apple wine, juice, or cider so that the honey dissolves. Float the orange, lemon, and cinnamon on top. Serve hot if you need blessings to come quickly, or cold if you need some time to cope more effectively with the situation as it presently exists.

Celebration Cup

Once your financial luck finally changes and you are back on solid ground, take a moment and celebrate that wonderful transformation. Pat yourself on the back for work and magic well done while enjoying this punch.

- ½ quart strawberries, sliced
- 2 peaches, sliced
- 1 cup fresh pineapple
- 1 cup maraschino cherries
- ½ gallon sangria
- 1 liter champagne (peach if available)
- 1 cup peach juice

Get out your favorite punch bowl and place about four cups of crushed ice in it. Put all the ingredient s over the ice and stir clockwise, saying:

> *"My thanks to Spirit for my blessings today,*
> *For helping me succeed and opening the way.*
> *Now continue to bless and watch and guide,*
> *In my heart, your magic abide."*

Drink out of your best champagne glass with friends and loved ones who can join in your celebrations.

Fun Adaptation: Want some other fun and easy beverage options? Just walk down the juice and soda-pop aisle of the supermarket! Drinks come in all flavors and colors these days, many of which will suit your magical goals perfectly. Get creative!

Foods

Cooking has always been a kind of mini ritual where we follow the same process every time for a successful outcome. Now all you're doing is adding a little magical energy to an already functional equation! You will be happy to know, however, that working with food is no different than beverages in the sacred kitchen. It might just require a little more planning (such as a trip to the supermarket for the right ingredients). Mind you, if you can find ready-made foods that fit your needs, those are fine too (just remember to bless them first).

Here are some recipes to get you started, but if you look at the component list at the beginning of this article, I think you'll find plenty of other favorite foods that you could use to motivate your monetary abundance.

Fertility Fish

Something seem a little fishy? Can't seem to get your life flowing in a positive direction that results in abundance? Well, let fish help you clear the path for success! Fish appears regularly as a sacred food among gods and goddesses of fecundity, including Ishtar and Atargatis. This is best prepared on Friday, the sacred day for all such efforts. Serve it with plenty of water, which represents life and positive movement.

- 1 tbs. butter
- 3 tbs. diced red onion
- 1 tsp. fresh garlic, chopped fine
- ½ cup sparkling white wine
- 1 mango, peeled and pulped
- ½ cup chicken stock
- ¼ cup light cream
- 1 tsp. lime juice
- Salt and pepper to taste

- 2 ¾-inch mahi-mahi steaks (or another of your choosing)
- Vegetable oil
- Lime (garnish)

Sauté the onion and garlic in butter until the onions are lightly browned (if you feel creative, pattern these in the frying pan so they look like a dollar sign). To this, add the wine and cook over a low flame until the entire mix is reduced by two-thirds. Pour this into your blender, adding the mango and chicken stock. Begin blending slowly, adding the cream, juice, and spices. Return this to your original pan and cook it down so that there is one cup of sauce total.

Take out your fish steaks, rinse them in cold water, and gently score them crosswise so the sauce will get inside as you grill. As before, get a nice even fire going on your grill and oil the rungs so the fish does not stick. If you have a vegetable basket, it helps to cook fish steaks inside so they don't fall apart.

Put the fish on the rack, turning regularly. It won't take long for these to cook, so you'll want to begin brushing them lightly with the sauce after the first turn. As when making the sauce, brush this on in a special pattern that represents your goal. The fish will be done in about ten minutes. Serve with more sauce poured over the top and a side of asparagus or other favorite vegetable.

Serve this dish just before undertaking any effort aimed at creating plenty. Just make room for whatever you wished otherwise you'll be caught holding a whole lot of "fish" without any place to put it!

Fun Adaptation: Substitute pineapple for the mango for an abundance of hospitality.

Productive Corn-n-Rice (serves two to three as a side dish)
Much like corn, rice brings you energy for both good fortune and profuseness with every grain. Corn is one of the "three sister"

crops, alongside bean and squash, which creates an abundant, self-sustaining garden, and the corn plant is a symbol of luck in some Asian countries.

- ¾ cup sweet, cooked corn
- 1 tbs. olive oil
- 1 small onion
- 3 tbs. white rice, cooked and hot
- 3 cloves garlic
- 1 green pepper
- 1 tbs. butter
- ¼ cup coriander leaves, chopped
- Salt and pepper to taste

You might want to pre-prepare this dish at dawn, which is the best time for magic for hopeful new beginnings. As the first rays of the Sun greet your ingredients, feel the warm renewing power there, and let that saturate both you and the food.

Chop the onion and garlic, and then slice the green pepper into a frying pan. Brown these with the butter and olive oil. Stir into the rice and corn (mixed together) with the freshly diced coriander leaves, and salt and pepper to taste.

Serve this dish prior to starting a new project that you want to see become immensely successful. Eat expectantly.

Fun Adaptation: Sprinkle with hot sauce for zeal in obtaining your abundance.

Bountiful Beer and Cabbage (serves six to eight)
Want to make it easy for abundance to find you? This blend is a good place to start. It relies on the cabbage and the zesty spices for its manifesting energy. The cream smooths the way for all the right transitions so that abundance can slide in unhindered.

- ½ pound bacon bits, freshly cooked
- 1 cup onions

- Ground pepper
- ¼ cup hot mustard
- ½ head shredded cabbage (red and green mixed)
- 2 cups dark beer
- ½ cup heavy cream

Save some of the drippings from the bacon in which to lightly brown the onions and pepper. Chop or slice the onions, visualizing any barriers between you and your desire being neatly chopped away, perhaps saying:

"I cut away my tears, I cut away my fears,
I cut away the obstacles that block energy.
Let abundance now flow free!"

Add the mustard, cabbage, and a little salt, sautéing for five minutes. Pour in the beer and cook for an additional twenty minutes, stirring regularly. Add the cream, covering the pan for ten minutes before serving.

Eat this particular dish right before a confrontation about something you perceive as slowing or deterring your efforts for abundance.

Fun Adaptation: This is quite tasty with a little pre-cooked, shredded corned beef added in, along with the cream. This particular variation inspires an abundance of luck!

Resource Spinach (serves five to six as a side dish)
Spinach comes to us from Persia, having arrived in Europe around the eleventh century. Its green leafy nature is ideal for money diets because it looks so much like currency. In this case, the idea is to protect one's resources and keep what you already have from dwindling.

- 2 1-lb. boxes frozen spinach
- ¼ cup olive oil

- 4 garlic cloves, chopped
- ¼ cup pine nuts
- 1 ½ tbs. balsamic vinegar
- ⅓ cup large pitted black olives, sliced

Warm the spinach in a large pot of water until slightly tender, then drain completely.

Warm the olive oil in an iron skillet, adding the garlic and pine nuts, stirring until golden brown (bear in mind that heat helps activate the magic in food). Pour in the drained spinach with vinegar and olives and continue stirring until warmed through. Place your wallet or other symbol of personal resources on the table while you eat, focusing the energy of the food toward them. This is a good time to add an incantation:

> *"Resources kept safe, resources hold,*
> *Resources wrapped in a protective billfold!"*

Fun Adaptation: Change the olives to green and add a smattering of alfalfa sprouts as a garnish for more moneymaking energy.

Opulence Onions (serves four to six)
Each layer of the onion in this dish surrounds and protects your magic and becomes a magical mandala to safeguard your treasures. It is also a symbol of eternity, meaning your opulence will last whenever it arrives.

- 6 large onions
- ½ pound shredded cabbage
- 2 garlic cloves, minced
- 1 tbs. olive oil
- Salt and pepper to taste
- 1 cup water
- ½ tbs. cornstarch
- ½ cup chicken broth
- 2 tbs. grated Parmesan cheese

Peel the onions, cutting off the ends so they will sit up in the pan. Clear out the center of the onion, leaving at least ⅓-inch thickness to create a shell for the filling. Keep about ¼ cup of the onion for the filling and reserve the rest for other cooking projects. Keeping your vegetable ends and pieces also supports frugal goals!

Using a steamer, tenderize the whole onions over boiling water for about fifteen minutes. While they cook, sauté the ¼ cup of onion remnants, garlic, and cabbage in a frying pan until lightly browned. Add the water, continuing to cook until the cabbage is tender and translucent.

Stir the cornstarch mixture with the chicken broth, adding it to the cabbage blend. Simmer until thickened. Finally, add Parmesan cheese and salt or pepper to taste. Use this to fill each onion shell, visualizing stuffing your pockets with money as you fill the onion and saying:

"Full, full, full,
May wallets and pocket ever be full,
Not for power, nor for greed,
But simply to meet financial needs!"

Fun Adaptations: It might be fun to use red onions for health-related investments, cooking onions for culinary investments, and perhaps white onions for emerging markets.

Financial Security Chicken and Spinach (serves two)
The spinach is the monetary ingredient in this recipe; the spices, red onion, and mustard provide protection; and the black-eyed peas bring a little luck for good measure.

- ½ cup dried black-eyed peas
- 2 chicken breasts, cut in strips
- 1 small red onion
- 1 tbs. flour
- 2 tsp. crushed garlic

- 1 cup chicken stock
- 1 cup shiitake mushrooms, sliced
- ½ pound spinach (or broccoli) finely diced
- 1 tbs. olive oil
- ½ tsp. thyme
- ½ cup sour cream
- 2 tbs. cooking sherry or red wine
- ½ tsp. spicy-sweet mustard

Security has a lot to do with the conscious mind, so you might want to prepare this dish at noon (or start it then) to accent logic and sound thinking. Soak the black-eyed peas overnight until tender. Note that these look like little eyes, providing the symbolic value of being able to recognize financial potential when you see it!

Finely chop the onion. In a large iron pan, sauté the onion with the garlic using a dab of olive oil. To this, add the mushrooms and thyme, cooking until tender. Add the sherry and remove from the heat.

Mix the flour with salt and pepper, then dredge the chicken strips in the blend. Using another frying pan, heat the remaining olive oil and brown the chicken strips, turning frequently to ensure even cooking. To these add your chicken broth, mushroom blend, and black-eyed peas. Cover for about twenty-five minutes until everything is heated through and the peas are tender. Add the mustard, spinach, and sour cream, continuing to cook for about four minutes, then serve it up hot (just as you want your financial tips and opportunities to be "hot").

Fun Adaptation: For even more security, add some cayenne pepper or Cajun seasoning to your dredging flour.

Prosperity Peas (serves four)
The best thing about prosperity peas is that they inspire wealth without costing you a fortune! At one time in history, these little vegetables were considered a traditional Witch's food.

- 1 lb. frozen baby sweet peas
- 1 lb. snow peas
- ½ lb. sliced bacon
- 2 shallots
- 1 pound pasta (your choice)
- Shredded cheese (your choice, for garnish)

Dice the bacon and shallots. Cook the peas in boiling water until tender, removing them from the water immediately and setting them aside. Next, sauté the bacon (Canadian style is nice) until crispy, reserving a little fat to sauté the shallots. If there isn't enough fat, or you'd like a less greasy alternative, use a little olive oil.

Meanwhile, bring a large pot of water to boil for the pasta. Drain when tender, then toss with the bacon, shallot, and pea mixture. As you mix these together, try an incantation:

> *"Pasta and pea, bring money to me!*
> *By bacon and shallot,*
> *Help me keep what I've got!"*

Serve with cheese on top.

Fun Adaptations: Use spinach noodles to support the money energies in this dish, or carrot noodles to give you sound insights on spending money wisely.

Providence Salad (serves three)
Luck comes in many forms, and sometimes we all need just a little boost to "get by." Rather than hoping for providence to find you, try this dish and generate some good vibrations yourself!

- 1 cup brown rice (cooked)
- ¾ tsp. salt
- ¼ cup red wine vinegar
- 2 tbs. olive oil (preferably extra-virgin)

- 1 tbs. grated Parmesan cheese
- 1 cup shredded, cooked pork
- 1 cup baby peas, cooked lightly (not too soft)
- ¼ cup chopped red onion
- 1 plum tomato, diced
- 4 oz. sliced olives

Once the rice is cooked, transfer it to a large salad bowl. Mix together the salt, vinegar, olive oil, and cheese. Toss this with the rice so it's evenly coated. Sprinkle the pork around the outer edge of the bowl, followed by inner rings of peas, onion, tomato, and olives. As you make each circle, say the following incantation four times (the number of Earth, which is the source of providence along with Spirit):

"Protect what I have, provide what I need."

This effectively creates a mandala of fortune, expressing your desire to the universe in visual form. Serve while still warm for fast results.

Fun Adaptations: Use black olives in this recipe to give providence and luck a firm foundation in which to grow. Green olives accent luck in a stressful situation (to bring peace) or for matters of personal growth.

Bring Home the Bacon (serves four)
Where luck abounds, blessings are not far behind. This recipe inspires a little of both. It has a truly unique flavor to tantalize your taste buds and your magic! It's also deliciously easy to prepare.

- 8 12-oz. preserved kumquats in syrup
- 1 tbs. honey mustard
- 1 tbs. real maple syrup
- 1 lb. very lean bacon (your favorite)

Pre-Spell Note: The symbolic value of this dish is increased if you can bring home the bacon for it just prior to preparing it, along with some cash in hand.

Place the kumquats with their juices, honey mustard, and maple syrup in a blender set to high. In a deep oven pan, lay out the bacon side by side, pouring the kumquat blend over top. Cook at 325 degrees for thirty to forty minutes. Serve as part of a blessing breakfast or as a side dish for a luck-encouraging dinner.

Fun Adaptations: You can use any fruit in this dish whose flavor you happen to like with bacon. Try using a whole diced orange with a cup of juice for luck in attracting wealthy mates, pineapple and juice for blessings when trying to borrow money from friends, or peaches in juice so that your providence is long-lasting.

Rice and Cabbage Consolation (serves two)
When life seems to have handed you nothing but bad luck, it's nice to have a good warm meal as consolation. This dish fits that task, and it adds a whole bunch of fortunate fare into your system to help turn things around and get you in the black again.

- ½ cup rice pilaf
- 1 cup broth (your choice)
- 4 slices lean bacon, cooked and drained
- 1 small red onion, diced and sautéed
- 1 cup shredded red cabbage
- 1 cup red beans (cooked)

This is really a very easy dish to prepare. Cook the rice pilaf in your choice of broth until it's tender. Crumble in the bacon, then mix with the onion, cabbage, and beans. Serve warm or cold with a bit of vinaigrette dressing, or butter and salt.

Warmth stimulates energy for change; a cold serving helps keep your head cool while handling the difficulties. Those shouldn't last too much longer after this meal. however!

Fun Adaptations: As with other recipes, you can change the color of the beans to better suit your goals (as well as the color of the cabbage). Use green cabbage (to represent greenbacks, and maybe even wear a green shirt on your back) and black-eyed peas for more insight into using what resources you have presently.

Opportunity Pears (serves two to three)
Instead of waiting for opportunity to knock, use this dish to open opportunity's door. After you walk through, the anise in this recipe safeguards your choice so the result is beneficial to both your finances and your self-confidence.

- 2 cups red wine (dry)
- ⅔ cup brown sugar
- ½ cup orange juice
- 1 tsp. ground anise
- 2 large pears, peeled, halved, and cored

Warm the wine with sugar, orange juice, and anise. Bring to a low rolling boil, then turn down to simmer for fifteen minutes. Add pears and continue cooking until they are tender. Let the liquid continue to reduce to a syrup stage (another thirty minutes). Serve hot if you want to stimulate a really "hot" opportunity, or cold for a more gradual change that you'll have time to seriously consider. If possible, use this bit of spellcraft to improve the results:

> *"Open the way, open the way,*
> *Opportunity knock (knock on something),*
> *All hindrances unblock.*
> *Open the way, open the way,*
> *I claim my chance beginning today!"*

Fun Adaptation: For the wisdom to choose between equally good opportunities, use apples instead of pears, or a combination of the two fruits.

Quick Cash Cabbage (serves four as a side dish)

This dish originated in Germany, where it is consumed during the Christmas season to inspire abundance, especially in the areas of good will, kinship, and welcoming. Better still, cabbage protects your abundance once it's obtained!

- 1 small head of cabbage
- 4 cups sangria or sweet red wine
- 1 tsp. cinnamon
- 1 tsp. salt
- 2 tbs. butter
- 2 tsp. sugar
- 1 apple, grated

If you can't wait until Yule to make this dish, create it when the Sun is high in the sky because Yule celebrates the return of the Sun to the sky and the lengthening of days.

Slice the cabbage and put it into a large bowl with the wine, as well as the cinnamon and salt, allowing it to soak overnight (at least eight hours) and mixing regularly. Drain, reserving the liquid.

Melt the butter in a frying pan, transferring the shredded cabbage into it. Brown gently, sprinkling the sugar over top to help caramelize the mix. Return the wine blend to the cabbage and simmer for another fifty minutes. Add the apple and cook for fifteen more minutes.

Put your debit card under the placemat or napkin while you eat this dish so it can absorb energy and provide you with cash quickly when you need it!

Fun Adaptation: If you're not fond of apple, this is actually quite tasty with sliced carrots. You will want to steam the carrots to firm-tender stage and add them during the last fifteen minutes of cooking as you would the apple. The carrots will help you keep an eye on your finances too!

There are many ways to enjoy food magic other than through recipes. Look at the names of various food products. Many of them have meaning there already! And, of course, if a food has special meaning to you, trust that meaning in your pantry enchantments. One of the greatest figurative sources of wealth which we have is our own experience. When you look to that, see what inspires and motivates you, and then apply that idea throughout your life, prosperity will naturally follow on all levels of being.

Chapter Three

ABUNDANCE AROMATICS

"Ointments and perfume rejoice the heart."
—The Bible, King James Version, Prov. 27.9

The art of aromatherapy has become very popular. Because no one thinks anything of entering a room and smelling a scented candle, air freshener, cologne, or potpourri, aromatherapy has the potential of being a marvelously subtle, nonintrusive form of magic that you can learn to use anytime, anywhere. Nonetheless, before I begin sharing some specific recipes for abundance aromatics, I'd like to explain a little of why aromas were and are connected to the magical arts.

If we turn back the pages of time for a moment, we will find priests and priestesses around the world offering incense to their gods and goddesses to please them and as a way of insuring Divine favor. By 1500 BCE, Egyptian healers and priests were already using aromatics for double duty: namely, lifting prayers to the heavens while also lifting a patient's spirit! The Greek healer Hippocrates studied aromatherapy diligently, and he felt the results of these studies proved that scents could be very beneficial to specific human conditions. Combine this kind of nearly universal reverence toward aromatics with the folklore imported by merchants traveling from Arabia, China, and India, and you have an atmosphere ripe for magic!

These ancient, global roots for aromatherapy are also those for which most modern aromatherapists reach to derive their methodologies. This is also where we find dozens of metaphysical correspondences mingled liberally into nearly every treatise on the subject. The two most stunning examples of this amalgam that most people readily recognize are the uses of lavender for calming and reassuring and rose for inspiring love! Magically speaking, these two herbs are used for exactly the same thing today, and lavender oil continues to be recommended by aromatherapists for easing stress.

What does all this mean to a modern magical practitioner? Basically, it tells us that we have a nice nucleus of historically tested ideas and methods on which to base our quest for aromatic prosperity. Although this nucleus isn't as important as personal meaningfulness, there is a power to tradition that shouldn't be underestimated. The material here endeavors to mix and mingle that tradition with applications that I've found fun and functional. From this foundation, please use your creativity and instincts to invent other recipes and applications that really waft with the aroma of your very soul!

The Nose Knows

With background in hand, we can consider why aromas affect us as they do. The sense of smell is one highly overlooked by many of us until we have a cold and nothing tastes good (because we can't smell it), or until something smells really bad! Nonetheless, all of our senses add something to how we perceive the world, and they also affect our mental, physical, and auric state in magic. The mental and physical effects come through the sense (that is, smell), while the auric effect is produced when an aromatic's energy signature merges into our physical energy envelope.

Think for just a minute about the smell of freshly baked cookies or bread. Don't you find yourself getting a wee bit excited by that aroma, and even perhaps notice your attention heightened by it? This is an excellent example of an aroma affecting you mentally, emotionally, and physically (through an increased pulse rate).

Adding the magical dimension onto this effect isn't difficult. In this case, we choose the aroma for its mystical energies and effects, be that correlation a historical or personal one. For example, we might use an oil such as rosemary to help us remember a spell or to improve our focus, because that is the traditional mystical value for this scent. We might dab on some sandalwood to purify our spiritual vibrations before bending and moving magical energy around. But what about using an aromatic specifically for monetary stability? How exactly do we go about doing that?

First, don't limit your concepts of aromatherapy to simply applying the oils you see in stores. We can achieve a sensual cue to our smell centers through any number of mediums including incense, freshly cut fruits, household air fresheners, powders, herb bundles, and so forth. Beyond this, aromatic plants can be:

- Scattered
- Burned
- Simmered or boiled
- Tossed in your dryer
- Rubbed into candles (or added to the wax)
- Bundled into sachets
- Grown (for ongoing "living" energy)
- Used in cooking (which releases their aroma and allows you to internalize the associated energy)

Aromatic oils and creams can be:

- Dabbed on lightbulbs
- Added to pet collars
- Smeared on book covers (small amounts are fine)
- Rubbed into pieces of furniture

- Placed on windowsills and doors
- Poured into bath water
- Used for anointing your body

These two lists give you a lot of options for creating personal abundance aromatics that will fill your home with wonderful scents and saturate the space with magic, too!

No matter what medium you use for carrying the aroma to your nose, body, and spirit, you will first need to know what scents have traditionally been used for money-related matters. This correspondence list will get you started. Please note that I've taken customary symbolic values for the aromatics and applied them to specific financial situations for illustrative purposes:

Prosperity and Abundance Aromatics
- **Anise:** Stimulating energy, acts as a boost to your magical efforts.
- **Apple:** Productive use of your resources and improved outlooks. White apple blossoms are an excellent representation of the Goddess.
- **Basil:** Concentrating and staying on-task so you can get the literal or figurative pay off.
- **Berry:** Luck with money, general abundance, and happiness. Raspberry has additional protective value for safeguarding resources.
- **Cedar:** Clearing away negative financial situations, courage in coping with excess bills, and so forth.
- **Chamomile:** Preparing the way for change.
- **Cinnamon:** Improved influx of money and personal energy to meet any associated challenges that go with it.
- **Clove:** An excellent component for prosperity incense. Also helps figuratively heal a financial problem.
- **Frankincense:** Decreasing the stress that goes with monetary constraints. Good cleansing herb.

- **Geranium:** Changing outlooks and attitudes toward money—specifically how you handle it.
- **Ginger:** Settling down a tenuous financial situation.
- **Grapefruit:** Getting a fresh start with hope as an ally. Also, improved physical energy when you need to work extra hours to bring in extra cash.
- **Honeysuckle:** Overall prosperity. Also, psychic awareness in applying your money safely.
- **Jasmine:** General attracting energies (very useful if you need to get a loan approved by someone of your preferred gender). Also improved personal awareness of how you use your money.
- **Lavender:** Overall sense of calm and stability so you can deal with issues with a clear head.
- **Lemon:** A great pick-me-up aroma that clears out the old and welcomes new energy.
- **Lilac:** Conscious awareness about how to best apply your funds. Also, overall symmetry in your life.
- **Lime:** Making headway (often slow and steady) on a financially sensitive project.
- **Lotus:** Effective use of your money when applied to your spiritual life and progression (like opening the way for funds to attend an event). Also, preventing financial misfortune.
- **Mint:** Overall money herb.
- **Myrrh:** Turning away unwanted energies, especially poverty.
- **Orange:** Applying money with real flair and style.
- **Patchouli:** Keeping other people away from your money, including theft. Good herb to honor the God aspect.
- **Peach:** Wise use of whatever funds you have. Wishcraft for money, especially funds you want to last.
- **Peppermint:** De-stressing after trying financial problems.

- **Pineapple:** Encouraging a figurative open door when it comes to asking others for financial help.
- **Rose:** Balancing your budget and maintaining that balance in how you spend money. Also, money that affects relationships.
- **Rosemary:** Remembering where and how you spent money so you don't overdraw your account. A good all-purpose, conscious-mind herb.
- **Sage:** Discernment in how to best apply money for long-term results. Making hard financial choices.
- **Sandalwood:** Self-confidence in money matters. Clearing your aura for money magic.
- **Thyme:** Intuitive use of money. Also, a good herb to use if invoking the fairies to help you find something of value or get a good bargain.
- **Vetiver:** Transforming your aura or situation into one that encourages prosperity and abundance. Overall herb that motivates change.
- **Violet:** Controlling a situation where money is over-valued or it's going out too quickly.

Nosing Around for Aromatics

Many people ask me where to best obtain good magical aromatics. My suggestion is this: Wherever possible, go with a known source of organic herbs, oils, and incense (food cooperatives are one possibility here). Don't overlook the Internet as a potential resource, too. Places such as Frontier Herbs have marvelous websites where you can get all kinds of aromatics at reasonable prices (www.frontiercoop.com).

Another common question that comes up is cost. From a historical standpoint, some magicians felt the more expensive an item was, the more powerful it was metaphysically. This idea likely originated in offerings to gods and goddesses where the greater the sacrifice, the greater the rewards! Modern opinions on this vary, but my general rule of thumb is that when you can afford quality, get it; when you can't, improvise. From a purely pragmatic standpoint, good essential oils tend to bear a heftier price tag, but they also last longer. A diluted essential won't be as strong, but it's less expensive and still bears the same energy imprint as the original.

Synthetic oils pose other considerations. Although cost effective, a synthetic vanilla won't work the same in magic as a natural vanilla simply because the second comes from nature's storehouse. So, if you like a specific synthetic blend and decide you want to use it in magic, you should spend some time extending your senses and discern what type of vibrational imprint it contains. Does it make you think of work, romance, a long walk in the woods? Use the scent's symbolic keynotes in applying it magically.

When cost is really a factor, some oils and incense can be made out of store-bought ingredients. And, if you feel so inclined, you could even plant many aromatics around your home to literally surround yourself in prosperity!

Rich Recipes

Now for the fun part: making some abundance aromatics. In approaching what is effectively an extension of herbalism and culinary arts, bear in mind that this is still a magical process. That means that you should:

- Be mentally, physically and spiritually prepared to work magic (meaning don't be angry, tired, or otherwise out of center).
- Consider if you want to time the preparation process symbolically (for example, a waxing moon to encourage financial growth).
- Consider adding magical touches to your workspace much as you might have when making Prosperity Potions and Financial Foods.

- Seriously consider creating these items in a sacred space, perhaps your magical work room or a kitchen that's been properly cleansed and blessed. Cleansing doesn't mean making things pristine, but a well-ordered and well-contemplated magical workspace does seem to improve the energy flow.

- Invite any household or kitchen god or goddess that you follow into the process for both blessings and increased effectiveness.

- Familiarize yourself with the spell-recipe, making any personally meaningful changes.

- Gather all the necessary components, cleansing and charging them as desired (or as instructed by the spell-recipe). Note: This is a good time to see if any of your magical tools can participate in the effort, because they are already charged with your energy. For example, if you use a wooden spoon as a wand, it certainly would be suitable to use it as such in this setting.

- Maintain your focus throughout the preparation process so that the magical energy lodges itself where desired and needed.

- Conclude the process with hope and thankfulness and watch to see how the universe answers the spell. I only mention this because all too often I see spells manifest in people's lives and they don't realize it because it's not exactly what they thought would happen! Remember, the moving of energy must follow certain natural ebbs and flows, and not all of those are ones that we can anticipate!

Air Freshener (Wax Base)

This is a marvelously simple aromatic to make, and it doubles as a candle later on. To one cup of melted candle wax (choose your color so it matches your magical goal, such as green or gold for money), add about ten drops of essential oil and/or up to ⅛ cup finely powdered herbs and resins. Pour this into a lightly oiled mold (any heatproof container works).

Place a loop-shaped wick in the center of the wax as it cools, so you can hang it up afterward. Hang the air freshener in a sunny window where the Sun's heat will activate your magic and release the aroma placed therein to bless and energize your living space.

Air Spritz

This is one of my favorite things to make because it works wonderfully with the Air element. The basic recipe is ½ cup denatured ethyl alcohol, ½ cup water, and ¼ cup aromatic water and/or four tablespoons aromatic oils. All the ingredients must be placed in a spritz bottle (such as those for glass cleaner) and aged for about one month before using. Shake well before each application.

Adding the magical dimension to this recipe isn't difficult. I suggest creating a blend that's attuned to any one of the four winds (each of which has specific powers). To work with an Eastern wind (money for new projects or a new beginning), use aromatics such as anise, lemongrass, lily, pine, sage, mint, and lavender. To work with a Southern wind (money to help support family/relationships), use aromatics such as allspice, carnation, chrysanthemum, cinnamon, ginger, marigold, and citrus. To work with Westerly winds (money for health-related issues), use aromatics such as lemon balm, chamomile, heather, jasmine, lemon, lilac, myrrh, and violet. To work with a Northern wind (money for strong financial foundations), use aromatics such as honesty, honeysuckle, patchouli, primrose, and vetiver.

Bear in mind that the goals of each aromatic when blended with the wind noted can certainly vary. Each wind bears the energy of the elemental quarter with which it's aligned. So, a Southerly wind can also increase energy for job hunting, empower your passion for work, or renew physical strength so you can apply yourself fully to financially prosperous tasks.

Likewise, an Easterly wind can increase personal attention toward financial matters or your career, improve your outlooks about how to effectively handle money, and make you more intuitive in handling your finances.

The Western winds provide courage to withstand hard financial times, provide daring to take a chance with money, and also generally fertilize any seed money you presently have on hand. Finally, Northern winds encourage financial growth, overall sustenance, money for newborns, money for funerals, and cash that you'd like to apply toward a creative endeavor.

The next step is putting the recipe together with magical processes. Once you've made and aged the air freshener, you'll need to wait for a day when the wind is blowing from the direction that best matches your goal. To be certain of the winds, you can get a windsock or check your local weather channel. Next, stand with your back to the wind so it moves forward past you (this carries energy forward symbolically). Hold the spritzer in both hands, close your eyes, and focus on your goal. Spray the aromatic four times (the number associated with resources), allowing the wind to carry that energy outward. If you want, you can repeat an incantation each time. Label the spritzer for future use.

Bath Salts

To one cup of sea salt, add twenty-five drops of essential oil and/or up to ⅛ cup very finely powdered herbs (so they don't clog your drain). Remember to choose the oils and herbs for their magical properties so they match your goals, and if you wish, you can add food coloring to the salts for even more symbolism. Sprinkle this into your bathwater in an outward moving spiral as you express your wishes via a prayer or incantation. As you soak in the water, the bath salts and their aroma interact with your aura so that you get out of the tub cleansed and re-charged with the magic placed therein.

By the way, if you don't have salts available, you can simply bundle your chosen herbs into an old stocking and float them in the water for similar results. Combine this with some candlelight and meditative music and you have all the right ingredients for some truly magical moments!

Candles

Candle magic is among the oldest and most widely used form of Witchery, more than likely because it is inexpensive, simple, effective, and employs a readily available component: wax! Because most people I know are very busy, this aromatherapy method will not include recipes for making your own candles. If you'd like to consider that approach so the candles have more of your personal energy, you can find great ideas and applications in *Exploring Candle Magic: Candles, Spells, Charms, Rituals, and Divinations.*

Instead, we're going to combine the color of a candle with various aromatic oils for specific monetary goals. You can either store the candles in scented wrappers or dab oil directly on them just prior to magical workings. The former approach saturates the wax with aroma, but really both work perfectly well. To this basic process you can also add a symbolic carving on the candle itself that also represents your needs (such as a dollar sign).

The following is a color-and-aroma chart to use as a helpmate to choose the best combination for your goals:

- **Black:** Use this for closing deals, banishing poverty, and seeing any financial situation for what it really is (good or bad). Black combines nicely with the aromatics of clove, juniper, and frankincense (for the goal of clear sight, I'd combine one of these three with sandalwood).
- **Blue:** Use this color to highlight your creative ability with money and good instincts on using it. Additionally, blue encourages thoughtfulness with how one applies

one's resources. Combine blue with lavender, violet, and lilac aromatics.

◆ **Brown:** Use this to create strong financial foundations and a sense of monetary security by scenting the candle with honeysuckle, patchouli, or vervain.

◆ **Green:** Use this for nearly any money magic, especially those associated with luck in money. Combine this color with pine, vetiver, and primrose.

◆ **Orange:** Use this to motivate yourself slowly toward making personal changes necessary to either save or make more money. Combine this color with peach or pineapple aromatic oils.

◆ **Pink:** Use this color when you need to borrow money from friends or family or when you need cash for a health-related matter. Combine it with rose, amber, and lemon.

◆ **Purple:** Use this color when you need to impose your authority over how money is being used, or when you feel your psychic abilities toward everyday matters is wanting. Combine it with scents such as jasmine, thyme, myrrh, and sandalwood.

◆ **Red:** Use this to increase your energy for handling tasks or problems at hand, for victory and success, and for overall protection. Blend red with vanilla, rose, and patchouli.

◆ **White:** Use white candles as all-purpose items. They have the additional symbolism of safeguarding what you have, providing personal clarity, and improving balance (perhaps for balancing your budget!). Blend with sandalwood, sage, frankincense, and myrrh.

◆ **Yellow:** Use yellow candles when you need to be mentally sharp, when you need to apply your knowledge skills for making money, or when you need to talk about money matters effectively. Blend it with scents such as rosemary, anise, and orange.

Remember that the scent of a color is only one vibrational aspect. To this basic aromatic you can add another aroma that refines your goal. For example, if you're using a purple candle for financial authority and want to temper that with love, add some rose oil with whichever other aromatic you've chosen.

Once you decide upon the color and aroma, the next step is to put the candle in a fire-safe container. Dab on the oil if the candle isn't already scented, placing it around the center point of the candle. Concentrate on your goal, then light the candle to ignite the energy. Adding incantations at this point is helpful, and you should allow the candle to burn minimally to the point where you placed the oil and/or a carving. If the candle burns itself out, or burns all the way down, that's fine. Save the wax to be reused in future spells that have a similar goal.

Cream

This recipe is based on the original form of cold cream, which dates back to the Middle Ages. Begin with one cup of melted candle wax, to which you add one tablespoon of aloe (luck with money or protecting your assets), lanolin (encouraging gentle changes), or cocoa butter (a sense of happiness with what you have), and approximately ten drops of essential oil (chosen to match your goal). If you don't find that ten drops create a personally pleasing potency, add more oil a little at a time.

Beat this blend clockwise with a wooden skewer or something similarly disposable to create positive energy. Continue stirring until the wax cools completely and you have a creamy consistency. Store in an airtight container. Note that you can pick out the color of the candle wax for its symbolic value, too!

By the way, for those of you who would prefer not to make cream from scratch due to time constraints, you can simply find a commercially available unscented cream and add your own aromatic oils or powdered herbs to it.

Finger Bowls

This is a rather charming custom that was common over one hundred years ago at Victorian tables. Finger bowls are simply small dishes filled with aromatic water for cleansing (you guessed it) sticky fingers! What's nice about making these for money magic is that all of us handle our money when we put it away or use it. This allows the energy from the aromatic water to be transferred into our cash!

To avoid an oily texture, it's best to create herbal waters by steeping fresh or dried herbs in warm water until you achieve a personally pleasing scent. The basic proportion is about one cup of tepid water to one teaspoonful of each herb, strained after being steeped. You can mix and match any abundance aromatic for this purpose; repeat the process with fresh herbs if you find the scent isn't strong enough from the first steeping. Make sure to refrigerate the blend until it's time to use it; the waters last a few days only.

Incense

Although most people think of incense in a religious context, historically speaking it was used to deter disease, banish nasty odors in public and private places, and scent hair and clothing. In fact, our modern word *perfume* comes from the obscure Italian word *parfumare,* which means "to smoke through." For our purposes, however, we do want to bring the spiritual dimension to bear. If that happens to collaborate well with a mundane use, all the better for our budget-minded gurus!

For best results in making blends yourself, I suggest starting with ½ cup of an aromatic wood powder (cedar or sandalwood, for example). To this base, add no more than three other dried herbs, up to ¼ cup total. If adding oils, you should add only a few drops at a time, using no more than three aromatic oils, until you achieve a scent you like. Bear in mind that things smell different when they burn from when they're dry or wet. Also remember that if you're adding oil to your wood powder, you have to mix it thoroughly and make sure it dries evenly before burning.

Stir your mixtures clockwise to attract positive energy or counterclockwise to banish the negatives. Keep your mind wholly on your goal while you work and add incantations as desired. (As with the candle and color combinations, these examples are for illustrative purposes only. Always let your instincts guide your choices.) Here are some sample blends to consider for money magic:

- **Rowan wood powder base:** Rowan has strong psychic and protective energy, as well as the ability to remedy a bad situation. To this, add cinnamon, lemon balm, ginger, or lotus.
- **Oak base:** Oak itself is a money tree, with the additional energy of good luck and productivity. Add almond, mint, pine, or lotus oils to this base.
- **Mesquite base:** Mesquite resolves situations that are draining your resources (both financial and mental). Add rosemary, vanilla, myrrh, or violet to this base.
- **Sandalwood base:** Sandalwood helps manifest our wishes, protect what we treasure, and banish negative energies. To this base, add sage, violet, patchouli, or rose geranium.
- **Cedar base:** Cedar is ideal for clearing the way for new endeavors and as an overall money wood. Add clove, frankincense, jasmine, mint, and lavender to this base.
- **Pine base:** Pine provides growth-oriented energy, along with that for multiplying resources. It will also help turn around situations that are draining your finances. To this base, add bergamot, vetiver, vervain, and gardenia.

- **Willow base:** Willow makes excellent divinatory incense especially when you want perspectives on money matters. To this base, add cherry, hibiscus, meadowsweet orange, sage, and rose.

Aromatherapy Oils

Making your own aromatherapy oils isn't difficult, but it does take some practice and patience to get them to; potency that you like. The basic recipe is one part dry herbs (or two parts fresh herb) to three parts good quality oil. Place these ingredients in a double boiler over a low flame and simmer for two to three hours. Keep the top of the pot on while the mixture cools. If you find the resulting scent isn't strong enough, repeat the process with fresh herbs, then strain it off into dark, airtight bottles with specific labels. Generally, these oils have a shelf life of about six months.

Following is a list of base oils and herbs that promote prosperity:

- **Almond oil:** Almond oil has a wonderful texture for massage, and the almonds from which it comes already bear the energy of abundance and wisdom. Blend this base with bayberry, pine, mint, sage, or violet.
- **Coconut oil:** Coconut oil solidifies when it cools, so it makes an ideal traveling blend. The base energies here protect your treasures and investments. Blend this base with myrrh, rosemary, geranium, or wisteria.
- **Olive oil:** Olive oil is one of the longest-lasting multipurpose oils that promotes situational healing, a sense of peace about where your next paycheck is coming from, and overall productivity. Blend it with carnation, vanilla, gardenia, rose, myrrh, or narcissus.

- **Saffron oil:** Saffron is the herb of kings, and it helps you live like a king even on a peasant's budget. It also promotes overall happiness. Blend it with apple blossoms, lavender, lily of the valley, and meadowsweet.
- **Walnut oil:** Walnut oil helps with wish manifestation and overall mental keenness for handling your situation effectively. Blend this base with honeysuckle, lilac, rosemary, sage, and violet.
- **Vegetable oil:** Vegetable oil has a fairly long shelf life, but not everyone likes the texture. Generally, it accepts aromas fairly readily, but not as well as olive or almond oil. Magically, it promotes strong foundations and is best blended with earthy aromatics.

Potpourri and Strewing Herbs

Potpourri and strewing herbs or plants are made from larger pieces of aromatics mixed into a personally pleasing and meaningful blend. Barks, dried berries, peelings, petals, pods, leaves, and even tiny branches might be included in your choices. To this foundation, you may add a hint of essential oil to improve the overall aromatherapeutic quality. Put all your components in a large mixing bowl and toss gently to activate the energy.

Potpourri can be set out in decorative containers that also have symbolic value, such as a cornucopia to inspire profuse prosperity. Leave this container in a warm spot to increase the amount of aroma it releases. Potpourri can also be simmered on the stovetop so that the scent fills a whole room or house. Conversely, strewing herbs are those that you toss to the winds: for example, scattering rose petals at a wedding. Sprinkle these outside your home to protect that which you value or to attract abundance to your doorstep.

To make wishes with your strewing herbs, you might consider combining them with the winds, as described with the air spritzer mentioned previously. In particular, the North wind bears the Earth element, which is ideal for establishing sturdy financial foundations.

Powder

Powder has several applications. You can use it on your body or sprinkle it in your shoes; if prepared properly with baking soda, you can sprinkle it into rugs before vacuuming to eliminate room odors. The basic recipe for making powders at home is one cup base plus ¼ to ½ cup very finely powdered herbs, or about twenty-five drops essential oil. Should you choose to use oils, you will need to sift the powder afterward so it doesn't clump, and make sure it dries thoroughly before storing it in an airtight container.

Here are some sample bases and blends:

◆ **Arrowroot:** Arrowroot has long been considered a curative, specifically for poison. Applying this metaphysically, this powder base banishes the toxic effects of hard financial times. Blend this base with lotus, rosemary, sandalwood, vetiver, or gardenia.

◆ **Baking soda:** Baking soda absorbs negative energies in and around your life. It also has an uplifting, cleansing quality. Mix this with apple blossom, clove, jasmine, frankincense, or cinnamon.

◆ **Cornstarch:** Cornstarch smooths the way for prosperity and motivates better luck. Blend this with cinnamon, lotus, lilac, almond, bayberry, or bergamot.

◆ **Talc (unscented):** Talc is an all-purpose, energy-neutral base that will accept the vibrations of whichever oils and herbs you add to it.

Sachets

Sachets can be made in every size and shape, but the easiest type is one fashioned from a square of fabric finished on all sides, similar to a small cloth napkin. The nice part about using a square is that the shape itself augments your goal by providing strong foundations.

Into the center of that foundation, you tuck your wishes in the form of herbs, flowers, and spices. Then gather the edges together and tie them at least one-half inch in with a ribbon or string. By the way, I like to stuff this as full as I can without it overflowing when tied by a ribbon, because this too represents profuseness.

Sun Strands

As the name implies, Sun strands have herbs, flowers, citrus rinds, and the like bundled or sewn into them. This is done when the aromatics are fresh, so that you get the additional benefit of preserving the items by drying. Fresh herbs are easily tied into a long strand and should be placed in such a way that the leaves hang downward, collecting the most essential oil as they dry. Citrus rinds can be attached together by needle and thread.

No matter what combination you use, hang the strands off a curtain rod in a sunny window so that the associated scents fill your home, and the plant matter dries evenly. Bear in mind that the light of the Sun saturates the plant matter with energy for the conscious mind, blessings, guidance, and a sense of authority for whatever situations you face. Additionally, if the strands catch moonlight in the evening, that will provide a nice intuitive balance point to whatever products you turn these into.

Once your strands are completely dried, you can store them as is for potpourri, or you can grind and powder them for many of the other recipes provided.

Something's Cooking in the Kitchen

I mentioned earlier that aromatherapy could be applied to culinary arts. Besides the scents released when you add spices to a recipe and cook them, there are several things you can make specifically for use in the prosperity pantry. Here are just a few that I've tried in my own kitchen.

Butter

Although herbed butter will have a stronger aroma when it's warm, there's nothing that says you can't use it cold too. Remember that "more" in magic doesn't always mean better or more powerful. The vibration of a scent or the herb that creates that scent is still present even in minute quantities.

To one cup of softened butter, add up to two tablespoonfuls of finely chopped herb (depending on personal tastes) and/or fruit juice. This has a very long shelf life, just as butter does, both in the refrigerator and freezer. Two blends that I like are apple-orange butter with a hint of cinnamon on a bagel (the circular nature of the bagel helps keep your magical energy moving) and sage-rosemary butter for basting chicken (symbolizing "healthy" bottom lines).

Oil

I love making flavored cooking oils. They make great gifts, look lovely in the kitchen, and serve several culinary functions (marinade, salad, sautéing, and sauce). Also, the symbolic value of saturating an oil with energy is very potent thanks to the process of steeping the herbs or leaving them in the bottle to continue the magical process.

I generally suggest using fresh herbs for your savory oils. Get whole cloves of garlic to protect your possessions, several large sprigs of dill for money, a little celery seed for mental clarity, and a hint of lemon rind so your abundance lasts. Place these in a pretty glass bottle for which you have a good top, then pour over some warmed peanut oil or olive oil; peanut oil in particular supports financial goals. This generally has a shelf life of four to six months. If the oil starts looking cloudy, discard it, because that means it's turned, and the magical energy likewise turns.

Savory Salt

Savory salt is deliciously easy to make. Just add any amount of finely powdered herbs to your table salt or finely ground sea salt. You can adjust the proportions in any personally pleasing way. Some combinations that I like are orange rind with garlic and ginger (particularly good for prosperity buffets), lemon rind with pepper and thyme (this clarifies your intuitive sense about money), and onion with basil and oregano (this helps manifest funds for supporting a relationship).

Sugar

Sugar accepts aromatics very nicely. In particular, placing a whole vanilla bean in your sugar canister results in a lovely flavor and aroma that's suited to most baking efforts. Vanilla magically promotes a clear head and improved mental energy for dealing effectively with your finances.

Another option is dried orange or lemon rind. Orange improves your luck with money, and lemon helps you stretch your resources for as long as possible. In using rinds, make the pieces large enough that you can easily separate them from the sugar. One to two one-inch-square pieces should suffice in a quart canister.

Vinegar

Savory vinegars are made exactly the same way as oils, except for the base. Here are some of the most popular vinegars from which to choose:

- **Balsamic vinegar:** Use this base to heal a difficult financial situation, or to help you recoup your hope and optimism with regard to financial troubles. Combines nicely with bay, garlic, rosemary, saffron, and thyme.
- **Red vinegar:** The color of this base provides overall energy. In particular, use this when you need a whole new start, or when beginning a new project that's going to impact your financial base. Combines nicely with ginger, celery seed, caraway, and savory.
- **Rice vinegar:** Rice represents the Earth's providence. It's an excellent overall money base, with the additional benefit of having productive energies. Combines nicely with basil, dill, marjoram, onion, poppy seed, and sesame.
- **White vinegar:** A pure, neutral color, white also stresses clarity. It is a sacred color to the goddess and therefore could be used to heighten any feminine characteristic of which you have need in your money matters (such as intuition). Combines with lemon balm, cardamom, lemon rind, and thyme.
- **Wine vinegar:** Wine has a playful, celebratory spirit. As a product of grapes (the fruit of the vine), it readily represents abundance and specifically prosperity that's worthy of a party! Good fortune and success are in this base. Combine with celery, caraway, rosemary, savory, and mint.

Chapter Four

WEALTHY WIZARDRY

*"Those who obtain riches by labor, care, and watching,
know their value. Those who impart them to sustain and extend
knowledge, virtue, and religion, know their use."*
—Charles Simmons

Even one hundred years ago, it was common to turn a silver coin
in your pocket by the new moon to turn money your way! Did
those people enacting such traditions think them magical or a
type of spellcraft? I doubt it. At that time, many superstitions
had magical overtones but were simply accepted as part of life
and culture. I think we might learn something from this example.

Spellcraft is an important part of a Witch's tool kit, but it
should not be seen as something supernatural. In fact, white
magic is constrained by the laws and patterns in nature. In other
words, our goal is to work *with* the universe rather than try to
swim upstream, against a natural energy flow. For one thing,
it is much easier and more ethical to take this approach. For
another, the results are usually far more pleasant and satisfying.

To help you understand what I mean, visualize a simple
square. Now, you can erase the lines of that square and draw

something else from scratch, or you can simply draw another image within, over, or around that square to change the pattern. For example, draw another square of equal size, tilted on one edge (a diamond), over the original. You now have an eight-pointed star. This illustrates the essence of spellcraft very nicely. A properly designed and executed spell creates a pattern that you add to the existing one. This, in turn, shifts the energies toward your goal without breaking natural law.

With this in mind, several questions become apparent: What pattern do you presently have, and what design or execution is best for transforming that pattern to one of prosperity? I won't tell you this is an easy question to answer, but it is one well worth pondering in your quest for abundance.

Each person's situation has different underlying vibrations. One person experiencing financial restrictions might be caught in a pattern that looks like a counterclockwise or downward spiral, for example. Another person's financial frustrations might come from a heavily laid pattern, often one that originates in personal habits, which resists change; this metaphorically looks like the black and white outlines of a coloring book in astral reality. Only you can determine what type of energy patterns are causing your difficulties; that's the bad news. The good news is that you can use a variety of spellcraft to help transform those patterns.

Forms of Spellcraft

Spellcraft takes many forms. Some spells have nothing more than a verbal component called an incantation. These types of spells work very well when combined with the Air element because sound is carried outward from you with the winds and your own breath. So, if you choose to contrive your own verbal spells, you might want to refer to *Air Spritz* on Page 54 for more ideas on how to combine the Air element with your incantation.

Keep in mind that the symbolic significance of "shouting into a wind" or "putting your back to the wind" —that is, resisting a type of energy has real merit here.

Spells can also be written or drawn. In this case, the words or designs in the spell provide the pattern for the energy to follow. One of the best historical examples of this is the old charm *abracadabra,* which was written in the form of a downward pointing triangle to heal a sickness. Not only did the word visually disappear, but it also translates into the phrase "perish like the word." In this manner, the ancient spellcrafters used the correct word and pattern so that the power of disease would shrink into nothingness.

The third form of spellcraft uses components-herbs, flowers, candles, crystals, photographs, and so on-to create an energy pattern. Exactly what happens to those components depends on the spell's goal. For example, someone wishing to halt negativity coming from another person might put a picture of that person in the freezer, literally freezing the negativity. Or someone making a devotional potion for a marriage ceremony might use rose petals picked in the light of the Sun to encourage love and blessings.

No matter the goal, the keys to success here are that the component's energies blend together harmoniously and that the manner of their preparation matches the theme of the spell. For example, I don't often recommend using a roaring fire as a component in money magic, because you don't want your cash to go up in flames! Now, you could toss some prosperity herbs on low-burning coals to lift your wishes in the smoke to the universe but burning them quickly away has the wrong symbolic value.

Finally, spellcraft often combines its base form with one of the four elements. Previously, I spoke about combining verbal spells with the Air element. Written and drawn spells combine nicely with the Earth element, which is also ideal for money magic. The component approach to magic has the advantage that it can be combined with any or all of the elements as follows:

- **Air:** Tossed into a wind, blown upon, smudged.
- **Earth:** Buried or planted.
- **Fire:** Burned or heated.
- **Water:** Floated on, frozen in, asperged.

When doing this specifically for prosperity magic, the Air element provides fresh ideas for moneymaking and also supports new endeavors. The Earth element brings growth and foundation-oriented energies, which is a nice combination when choosing long-term investments. Fire can destroy a negative or heat up a financial opportunity that's grown cold. Water improves the overall flow of money into your home and life.

I will be providing specific spells for abundance and prosperity in the material shared here. Beforehand, however, I think it is important that everyone on a magical path have a good working knowledge of spellcraft. Although this is a very basic overview, use it for reference when you'd like to adapt the spells in this or any book or design some of your own.

1. What is the focus of your spell? Can you narrow this theme down to a short word or phrase? For example, money magic has a lot of aspects: job security, financial flow, bottom line, balanced budget, credit lines, investments, and so forth. To what part of wealthy wizardry is your energy going to be directed specifically?

2. What form of spellcraft will work best considering this goal? If you're about to go to a bank and talk to a loan officer, for example, I'd suggest a verbal spell combined with one of

the four winds (East is a good choice for clarity of thought and communication). On the other hand, if you're trying to track your spending and saving, you might want to light a green candle with a dollar sign on it and have that burning while you work (the component form).

3. Do you want to blend forms for greater focus? Many component spells that you will read here and elsewhere include incantations and/or written elements. The more senses you can bring into your spellcraft, the better the results tend to be. Think of each sense as providing another dimension to the pattern you're creating.

4. Gather everything necessary to cast the spell and consider if you want to enact it at an astrologically beneficial time. Waxing moons, for example, support increase and full moons support sufficiency or abundance.

5. If you're using components, you may wish to cleanse them first using a sprinkling of saltwater or smoke: from a purgative incense such as sage. This eliminates any haphazard energy from the equation, which might change the pattern of the magic.

6. Cleansing is also often followed with a blessing that sets apart the item for its designated function. Blessings typically invoke a personal god or goddess but can also be directed to the Universal Source.

7. Cast the spell, bearing in mind that your thoughts and actions throughout the process create the energy pattern as much as the form and components chosen.

8. Release the spell. Don't hold onto the energy unless you mean to internalize it.

9. Ground yourself. Working magic can make you very light-headed, and because magic takes place between the worlds, it's good to get one foot in reality before driving! Eating meat or crunchy vegetables helps with this, as does simply sitting on the floor and breathing regularly.

10. Follow up the spell with concrete action in the mundane world. For example, don't cast a spell for a better-paying job and simply expect that one will appear out of nowhere. Get out your resume and read the classifieds so the universe has an opportunity to put your energy to work!

11. Make notes of your successes so you can re-create those spells in the future when a need arises. This is a kind of wealth in its own right.

Doesn't sound that daunting, does it? That's because spellcraft is a very old and beloved magical art that has strong roots among everyday people. Yes, it can get far more complex than this, but it need not be complicated to be meaningful, powerful, and transformative.

The next question people often ask me is if spellcraft has any rules. Yes and no. Among Wiccans, the phrase "do as you will, and it harm none" comes up regularly, but not all metaphysicians follow that guideline. What I will give you here are my rules. You will have to weigh them against your own heart and path to determine if they're right for you.

◆   If I can do it myself, without magic, I do! This kind of comes under the heading of "god/dess helps those who help themselves." I'd rather save magical energy for those times when I'm really at a loss. Hard work still makes good sense.

◆   If my motivations aren't what they should be, I wait. Always examine the bottom line. Need is different than greed, and the desire for change is different than manipulation. The phrase "know yourself" should always be part of a Witch's rule book.

◆ If I'm tired, out of sorts, sick, or feeling unfocused, I wait. All of these types of mental, physical, and spiritual conditions can affect spellcraft adversely.

◆ If I'm not willing to be wholly informed, discerning, aware, and accountable in the way my spellcraft is designed and cast, I don't do it. Irresponsible spellcraft is a myth. No matter how innocently contrived, each of us is responsible for the patterns we create or destroy by our magic, and we'd better be certain we're ready for the karmic implications here. This means not casting spells based on gossip or rumor and not casting spells with components or methods that go against personal guidelines.

◆ If I come across a spell that doesn't make sense to me, I either change it or don't use it. There are literally thousands of spells in this world, but not all of them work for all people! Each of us works with magic in a slightly different way, and we must learn to recognize the processes and components that truly harmonize with our spirit. Again: Know yourself, remembering that magic without meaning is nothing more than dogma and rote liturgy.

◆ If I am too personally involved in a situation to remain neutral, I ask someone else to help with the magic, or I avoid it. Magical energy is a neutral force, and you want your spells to be non-manipulative of others' free wills. Yet, we are human beings with failings, and sometimes remaining objective is difficult. When this happens, it's best to ask for help or wait until your head clears.

◆ Every spell I cast contains the phrase "for the greatest good and it harm none." This allows the universe to step into the equation and guide my energy in ways that will be most beneficial, where my vision might be wanting.

Again, I have to stress that these are rules that work for me. I think they are sound and wise, but ultimately you must be your own guru, priest, and priestess in applying such guidelines to your life.

Another question many people ask is whether or not you *need* to create sacred space for spellcasting. From a historical perspective, spells were done both within and without the protection of a sacred space. It has always been my opinion that each person's body is a temple and therefore a kind of portable sacred space that's ready when you are! I also feel that simple matters and day-to-day magics really don't require a fully formalized sacred space. I put money-related magic in this day-to-day category, except during times of great need.

That being said, having the magic circle set up correctly and fully activated when you're spellcasting has advantages. For one, it keeps out unwanted influences. For another, it holds your magical energy in place until you're ready to direct it toward the goal.

One good way to compromise is to visualize a white light sphere around you while you're crafting your magic to emphasize the temple of self-concept. It's not quite the same as formalized casting, but it requires much less time and effort. On the other hand, if you want to cast a formal circle, go for it! The more you enact protective, prosperous magic in your home or magical space, the more you saturate that area with good vibrations!

Spells for Prosperity

Money in a Month

Find a box of green or gold candles at an inexpensive outlet. On the first night of a full moon, carve each one of them with a dollar sign near the midpoint of the candle and dab it with mint oil. Light one of these every morning (at dawn is best to start a new cycle), saying:

> *"After a month, yes thirty days,*
> *Prosperity and providence shall have their way.*
> *A spark of hope, by dawn's first rays*
> *The spell's begun, the magic laid!"*

Let it burn in a safe place until you have to leave the house. Continue this every morning until the next full moon. Be sure to save your wax remnants for melting and making into money air fresheners.

Breakfast Bounty

When your finances are particularly tight, consume grain cereal every morning for breakfast. Eat from the edge toward the center, focusing on that point as being your financial goals. Visualize each bite being filled with a blend of sparkling gold light so you internalize the energy of abundance.

Anything with an oat, corn, rice, or barley base symbolizes providence. In ancient times, having these grains in your house meant the harvest was good, and therefore prosperity followed.

Treasure Protector

Safeguarding your valuables also protects your prosperity because you won't have to spend money to replace them! One way of doing this is by sprinkling caraway seeds into your wallet and other items that you want to guard against loss or theft. As you do this, say:

> *"Caraway keeps thieves at bay.*
> *My magic surrounds; protection abounds!"*

If you wish, repeat this incantation four times, the number of abundance, or eight times for completion (also double four).

Checkbook Candle

Take some of your remnant prosperity candle wax and re-melt it. To this base, add a bit of mint and pine. Let this begin to cool on the stove. Meanwhile, lightly oil the inside of an old, well-washed milk carton. Pour a little wax in the bottom (about an eighth of an inch) and let it cool to semi-solid. On top of this place a silver coin, along with one of your account balance receipts, deposit slips, or check stubs. Pour in the remaining wax, saying:

"Clear vision be mine. Wherever this candle shines,
Money grows. Prosperity flows,
Each time this magic candle glows!"

Add a wick (you can suspend this from the top of the carton by tying it to a pencil placed across the opening). Unmold when the wax has cooled completely, lighting the candle any time you have to pay bills, balance the budget, or do other financial chores that affect the bottom line.

Eggplant Essentials
Take a small eggplant and cut it in two. In the center of this vegetable, place a coin minted in the year of your birth. Wrap the coin with a piece of paper specifying the amount of money you need to get by (and only that much—no getting greedy!). Tie the two halves together using a green string; ribbon can harm animals, so be thoughtful toward the environment. Bury the eggplant in the ground with four seeds from a flowering plant above it. Care for this seed with diligence, focusing on the amount of money you need each time you water or weed. By the time the seed flowers, your wish should manifest.

By the way, an alternative to using an eggplant is to get a piece of ginger root and carve your need into it. Bury this in the same manner as the eggplant.

Power of Attraction
Take a piece of paper and write your need on it. Be specific: If you need a better job, say so! Wrap this around a small magnet, then tie the whole bundle to a string approximately three feet long. Place the bundle across the table from you with the other

end of the string in your hands. Stop for a moment, breathe deeply, and focus on your goal. Whisper:

"To me, to me, come to me!"

Begin to pull on the string so the bundle comes closer to you. Keep repeating:

"To me, to me, come to me!"

Allow your voice to become more commanding and stronger until the bundle reaches your hands. At this point, carry the bundle with you at all times until the spell manifests, then bury it with thankfulness.

Eggshell Spell
When money is slow in coming, take a fresh egg and salt to a crossroad. The egg represents potential; the salt, cleansing; and the crossroad, change. Break the egg, sprinkle it with salt, and bring the eggshells home with you. According to custom, the eggshells should be burned to speed the acquisition process. This is particularly useful in speeding up a loan or line of credit.

Bay Abundance
Get a large bay leaf and inscribe a dollar sign on it. You can do this with a marker, pencil, or your finger, which will rub your body oils into the leaf. Put this leaf in a very safe location until money begins to arrive. At this time, break up the leaf adding it to incense for continued prosperity, or simply burn it in thanks for Spirit's gifts.

An alternative approach is to take several large bay leaves with dollar signs on them and attach them to the brambles of a berry bush. When the wind carries them away, it also bears your wishes and releases the magic.

Rope of Riches

Knot magic was very common in ancient Arabia, and this spell is based on that tradition. Take seven one-dollar bills and a long piece of rope (a green or gold one, which you can get at curtain stores, is best). Tie each dollar separately into the rope, saying:

"Prosperity within release to begin!"

Hang this rope in your closet or another location where it won't be disturbed. When you need to release the energy of abundance, untie one of the dollars and give it to a good cause. Never undo the last dollar, however, because taking it implies greed and brings financial troubles. This should remain on the rope as seed money, and new dollars bound below it.

Lakshmi's Luck

In certain parts of Asia, people honor Lakshmi, the patroness of wealth, fortune, and prosperity. Anything that enriches life is under her dominion. To invoke her blessings on your home, lay out lotus petals on your altar with a white candle. If you don't have an altar, any tabletop will do. As you light the candle, say:

"Goddess of wealth, abundance, and joy,
I place before you your sacred flower.
As its gentle aroma fills my home,
So too fill my life with your fortune."

Let the petals dry completely, returning one to the Earth as an offering to Lakshmi and using the rest in abundance, luck, or productivity incense.

Hour Power

Much like crystals, herbs, and other ingredients, hours of the day have different magical correspondences. You might consider timing your wealthy wizardry by this clock to empower it further.

Adding to this symbolism, enjoy a bowl of fresh berries, the Earth's prosperity, with your dinner (around 5:00 p.m.) to internalize that energy and carry it with you through the rest of the day.

Billfold Blessing
Keep an eye on your money. When you see a one-dollar bill with the year of your birth on it, fold it in on itself four times saying:

"One for prosperity,
Two for fertility, three for luck.
God/dess, bless this buck!"

Keep the folded dollar in your wallet or purse to encourage wealth.

Clothes Make the Person
Buy yourself a new piece of clothing and before putting it on, say:

"Wealth to wear it,
Strength to tear it,
And money to buy another."

This invocation comes from an Irish blessing, where a person would be wished "health to wear" a new item of clothing. Recite this on the Spring Equinox for greatest power and repeat the incantation each time you wear the item in the future to support the magic further.

Garden Gold
If you enjoy gardening or even having a few potted plants around, consider planting some prosperity for yourself. Come spring, pick out gold- or yellow-colored flowering plants and add them to your gardens plentifully. As you sow the seeds or bulbs, say:

"By my hand, this plant I tend.
By my will, my wealth will mend.
As above, so below,
By this spell, my money grows!"

You can repeat the incantation each time you weed and water your garden gold. Then, dry some of the petals and use them for abundance aromatics.

Turning the Tide
Go to a nearby beach when the tide is low. Draw a large dollar sign or other symbol that represents your need more specifically, in the sand. Keep your mind firmly on your goal while you do this, visualizing your wishes in manifested form. Then, when the tide turns, it also turns your fortunes and takes your wish out to the four corners of creation in each wave.

May Wishes
Throughout the month of May, toss a coin or a green stone into any wishing wells or fountains you pass. Be sure to whisper your wish thrice first. The well spirit will see your offering and bless you with small improvements.

Periwinkle Providence
Bathe in saltwater on the first, ninth, and thirteenth nights of the Moon (the first night is the first time you can actually see a sliver of light from the lunar sphere). Afterward, go out and gather a handful of periwinkle blossoms. Make these into a small sachet that you carry with you, because it will attract divine grace and abundance.

Starlight Starbright
There are all kinds of wishing customs associated with stars, including ones for prosperity. For example, if you wait for

the third star to appear in the sky at night, place a gold coin in your left hand, and make a wish for wealth, it should begin to manifest within a month.

Rosemary Reward

Get a handful of fresh rosemary and bind the ends with green or yellow thread. Crisscross the thread around the bundle, making a wish for prosperity, money, success, and so forth at each cross point. You can tie the cross points with knots to enclose your magic. Hang this near the hearth to draw abundance into your home.

Money in the Moon

An old English custom instructs us to hold a silver coin to the sky when the Moon is new and say three times:

> *"May what I see increase,*
> *And what I suffer decrease."*

Carry this coin with you frequently thereafter until things improve. At that point, give the money to a good cause to pass along the blessings to another.

Turn It Around

When you find you're suffering an unusual number of setbacks, a great magical remedy comes to us from China. There they turn every mirror in the house, so it faces outward, reflecting away negative energy. Adding to this symbolism, you can also turn socks inside out, turn over an hourglass, turn your wallet upside down in your pocket, and so forth. This small action is based on the idea of patterning, discussed previously. Because you want to turn the trend around, start turning items around while focusing on the financial goals. You can add an incantation if you wish:

"Negativity turn, turn, turn.
I've money to earn, earn, earn.
Turn it around, ill luck is bound,
Prosperity found!"

Right things when the transformation starts being noticeable.

Dreaming of Money
Drink a cup of rose and/or marigold tea before going to bed and place a piece of paper with the symbol for Mercury, the messenger of the gods, under your pillow. Bless the tea by saying:

"Petals of prophesy, reveal to me,
The solutions to problems I cannot now see."

Go to bed, keeping a pad and pen or recording device nearby. Make note of any dreams or insights with which you wake up, because these will have clues to solving your financial woes.

A Mile in Your Shoes
This is a marvelously simple spell. Get some dried pear slices and powder them finely. Symbolically, this breaks down anything standing between you and your goal. Blend the pear powder with a little cornstarch and sprinkle your shoes with it daily so prosperity walks with you.

Wreath of Wealth
It's easy to make a wreath from grape vines, pine sprigs, wheat tops, dill flowers, and nuts. This should be hung in the kitchen, replacing whatever you use from it regularly, which symbolically replaces your money. The ingredients from this may be used for both culinary and magical purposes to fill everything with supportive energy.

Dandelion Divination

In the language of flowers, the dandelion represents an oracle. In this case, we're going to use it to determine how long your present financial situation will last. Take a dandelion gone to seed and hold it upright. Concentrate on your circumstances and blow on the head of the dandelion four times; this will carry the seeds on the wind, along with a wish for change. However many seeds are left represents the number of days, weeks, or months during which you can anticipate constraints.

Birch Blessings

Strips of birch bark were often used for paper when actual paper couldn't be found. They were also employed for magical words and images. In this case, write your need on a strip of bark gathered from the eastern side of a tree, where the bark is blessed by dawn's light. Float this on a stream moving toward you so that your fortune also moves your way.

Pocket of Prosperity

Save the pocket from an old shirt or pair of pants. Stuff this with vervain or pearl moss. When you need a consistent income, burn this in a fire-safe container or on a bonfire (during a waxing to full moon, if possible), saying:

> *"Ashes to ashes, dust to dust,*
> *Magic find your way and do as you must.*
> *On the winds, in the fire, my prosperity free!*
> *By my will and Spirit's blessing, so mote it be!"*

Keep a bit of the ashes from this fire for use in money charms and amulets.

Silver Water

On the night of a full moon, fill up a silver-toned pitcher with water. Put a silver coin into the bottom of it and go outside with the pitcher. Hold this in both hands, saying:

> *"Silver Moon, silver coin,*
> *In this water your power join.*
> *When taken within release in me,*
> *The power to attract prosperity."*

Make sure the reflection of the Moon is on the water as you cup your hands, gathering the Moon and the water in them, and drink deeply.

Rainy Day Fund
Take a green envelope and place therein four ten-dollar bills, saying:

> *"Bounty of Earth, sustenance here abides.*
> *I seal my magic spell inside,*
> *Kept safe until called by necessity,*
> *Then when opened, the magic is freed!"*

Seal this with green wax upon which you've drawn a symbolic rune, such as that for the Sun, which encourages bounty or one for protection to safeguard what you have. Put this in a safe place, opening it only when you have a desperate need and making sure to give at least one of the bills away to a good cause so that money returns to you threefold.

An Apple a Day
Carve words from a sacred text that promotes prosperity on an apple. One example is from The Bible, King James Version, Psalm 112.3: "Wealth and riches shall be in his house." Eat the apple to internalize the blessings. It helps the magic if you use a verse that's special to you somehow.

Flour Fulfillment
The next time you spill a little flour on the countertop, gather it together and put it in a cloth bundle with any silver- or gold-toned item, saying:

> *"Prosperity gathered within,*
> *By my will, this spell begins,*
> *That luck and fortune to me find their way,*
> *As I carry this through the day."*

Tie the bundle tightly but with a bow. Keep it with you, and when you really need luck or money situations to change quickly, sprinkle a bit to the winds, saying:

> *"I release my magic to the wind,*
> *And with it my message of need I send,*
> *Help this situation now to mend!"*

Tie the bundle back up and listen for opportunity to knock.

Keys to the Safe

Keep a key hung on a wall in your home. In those moments when you have gone to friends or family asking for financial aid and you want to know if the answer will be yes, look at the key. If it has rusted, the omen is positive.

By the way, you can use old keys, especially skeleton keys, as wonderful spell components because they symbolize unlocking the treasure trove in your life. Find one that you like and leave it in sunlight for four days, followed by three nights of the full moon's rays. Put it on your keychain after that, saying:

> *"Unlock the flow of fortune;*
> *Turn all bane and grant this boon.*
> *Unlock the door to riches,*
> *For such is the birthright of Witches!"*

You can repeat this incantation when you need to speed up manifestation.

Amber Abundance

Find an amber bead. In Greek mythology, amber was created from the tears shed by the daughters of the Sun, and it's a powerful stone for encouraging blessings. During the first or eighth hour of daylight, attach this bead to something that houses your money (a wallet, purse, or pocket is ideal), saying:

> *"Dollars and dimes, credit and cents,*
> *Bring to me wealth and opulence!*
> *That I shall never want, and money never wane,*
> *Bring me luck and financial gain!"*

This brings riches to the bearer.

Show Me the Money

When your finances seem to be on an even keel and you'd like to keep them that way, gather all the spare change and other cash you have in the house and bring it to your sacred space. Walk around this four times with your strong hand extended toward the pile, saying:

> *"I seek not riches nor greater gain,*
> *But to have and to hold, to hold and maintain!"*

Repeat the incantation once with each circuit, then put the loose change into a bank account where it can maintain its value.

Coconut Cash

Hollow out a coconut that's sliced in half. Fill one half with a mixture of coins, mint, lettuce, and a slip of paper on which you've written your present monetary goals. Seal the two halves together and cast the coconut into the ocean. The waves will wash prosperity back to you.

Saltwater is Sweet

An old spell instructs that you should take a container of saltwater to another source of running water, preferably when the Moon is full. Moving water is considered magically alive, and the full moon represents abundance. Hold the container of saltwater in hand while focusing on your wishes. Slowly pour out the water, seeing it filled with gold and silver light as it moves away from you to where your fortune lies. Some type of improvement should begin to manifest within a month.

Money Bath

At noon on any day in March (the month of success) or April (the month of good luck and opportunity), prepare a warm bath for yourself with patchouli oil and a cinnamon stick. Use the cinnamon to stir the water clockwise around yourself while you soak, saying:

> *"Money surrounds, luck abounds,*
> *In my aura, through all of me,*
> *I claim financial liberty!"*

Stay in the water as long as you wish, knowing that any negative energy that might be lingering about will be drained down the tub when you emerge.

Business Success

When you're travelling abroad on business, find a spot out in nature where you can gather some small stones. Once you have a good-sized handful, place these in a decorative pile beneath an oak tree or other very strong, vital bower. To empower this natural altar, you can leave a piece of your hair or spit upon the pile and say:

> *"As sure and strong as this tree,*
> *So too will this meeting be for me.*
> *Rooted in earth, and yet reaching for the Sun,*
> *By my will, this spell's begun."*

You can change the word *meeting* to *business success* or anything that better represents your goal.

Leave the pile where it is. If you return to this spot in the future, add a stone to the original pile or a sprig of fennel to reactivate the magic.

Ringing in Riches

Find a bell whose sound is pleasant to you and hang this somewhere near where you do your magic. Each time you do a prosperity spell, create a money charm, or perform an abundance ritual, make sure to ring the bell. This calls in aid from beneficent spirits, while neatly chasing away the bad ones!

To this basic process you can also add a reading from any book that is special to you and that also supports your goal somehow. I find that books such as *Bartlett's Familiar Quotations* (or the site www.bartlettsquotes.com) come in very handy, because many of the entries have a poetic or invocatory feeling about them.

Transformational Thresholds

It has long been a custom among various cultures to paint or engrave prosperous sayings on one's threshold to inspire that energy throughout the home and on everyone who walks through. Adapting that concept somewhat, look for a green or gold colored welcome mat or one that bears a clever saying that you could bless and empower for magic each time you pass by it. An incantation such as this might do the trick:

"Where my feet pass, let there be providence.
Where those of my friends and family pass, let there be love.
To my house, and all who come this way,
Grant the blessings of prosperity, health, and joy.
So mote it be."

Harvest of Your Labors

Take an egg and mix it with about ¼ cup of breadcrumbs and ¼ cup of flour. Stir this clockwise, saying:

"Staff of life, egg of possibilities, bless the tools of my trade
that I might use them effectively in support of my home and family."

Dab this mixture on whatever represents the tools of your trade (for me it might be a pen), then go to work!

Fertile Eggs

Among their other nutritional (and magical) properties, figs contain properties that can increase fertility. So why not give it a try for your money, too? Get some dried figs and rub your cash gently with a piece or two. Afterward, you can eat the fig to internalize the energy or return the piece to the Earth by way of an offering that anticipates success.

If you're not fond of figs, use orange bergamot oil or tea instead.

Crystal Clear

Take one round stone and one square stone and plant them in rich soil, saying:

"As yin to yang and woman to man,
Bless my heart, my home, my land.
That money grows and constraints wane,
Bring blessings to my life again!"

This spell is adapted from an idea put forth by ancient Greek philosopher Theophrastus, when he suggested that some stones were male and female, and if left in the ground long enough together, they would give birth to riches.

Turquoise Treasure

On the first night of a new moon (when you can see the first sliver of light), go outside with a turquoise in hand. Do not look at the Moon immediately. Wait until you're in a good position to be able to look at the Moon's light and then immediately at the turquoise. So doing, according to Hindu and Persian lore, brings immeasurable wealth.

Woodland Wealth

If you're out in the woods and happen across a wild hops plant, immediately take a coin from your pocket and place it in the earth near this plant's root. As long as it remains there and the plant thrives, so too will your fortunes.

Coin and Cork

British custom tells us to save the cork from any auspicious occasion (especially weddings), slice it, and put a silver coin into that slot. Keep this token to ensure your needs will always be met.

Final Notes on Spellcraft

You will notice that spells have a lot in common with charms, amulets, talismans, and fetishes. That's because all use similar processes to effect positive change. Additionally, many times the only thing that separates one from another is little more than jargon.

As you weave your wealthy spells and begin working on charms, I leave you with some advice. The universe has a wicked sense of humor and its own kind of checks and balances. So, expect the unexpected. Spellcraft will not always manifest in the way you anticipate, and often it does so with a healthy dose of humor in tow. This is simply a way that the universe keeps us honest, active, and aware as co-creators in our destiny.

Chapter Five

TREASURE TALISMANS

"Riches do not consist in the possession of treasures,
but in the use made of them."
—Napoleon Bonaparte

Who says you can't take it with you? Many of us carry charms and amulets to inspire other kinds of energy in our lives, so why not have one or two to safeguard and increase your prosperity on all levels of being? This information also includes fetishes for finding "treasure" (such as at flea markets), talismans for hunting down bargains, and other forms of thrifty Witchery aimed at keeping money where it belongs: in your pocket!

The Name Game

Before getting into making charms, amulets, talismans, and fetishes, it's very helpful to understand these terms. I believe that charms are the oldest form of portable magic, the first having been only verbal in nature. I'll explain more of the whys of my theory later, but it all begins with linguistics. The word *charm* comes from the Latin word *carmen*, which means "song, verse, or incantation." This meaning and original function explains why so many spells have a verbal component.

Defining a charm more specifically, it can be a word or phrase (often repeated a symbolic number of times), an object, or a symbol that has power (or has been instilled with power). This energy or power is active all the time, and it is usually designed to attract something positive to the bearer. Common themes for ancient charms include those for health, love, and wealth. In fact, we still see charm bracelets with little symbolic tokens on them; each token promotes something positive. These pieces of jewelry owe their origins to this concept.

Now, let's compare this information about charms to amulets. The word *amulet* comes from the Latin word *amuletum*, which Pliny the Elder repeatedly referred to in his book *The Natural History of Pliny* as "an object that protects a person from trouble or illness." This alone implies the strong links between the two magical processes. Today, amulet and charm can be used interchangeably in some contexts. The main difference between the two seems to come down to the way in which they work.

Charms are constantly active; amulets remain inactive until some external or internal force turns them on, rather like a light switch. Where charms attract, amulets protect, repel, and remedy. Finally, where charms were traditionally very simple in their design, amulets became far more complex in both their components and crafting methods. Start out with a perfectly good, working construct and someone, somewhere, will want to complicate it!

Talisman comes from the ancient Greek word *telein*, which means "to initiate into the mysteries." Typically, talismans were cut or engraved under specific astrological conditions. Different from both amulets and charms, however, talismans are considered active participants in magic, such as the rod of Moses, which represents transformative magic. As you read old folktales, you will notice that many a talisman's power came from a captured indwelling spirit. Aladdin's lamp is a prime example:

The only problem comes when that spirit gets difficult and doesn't want to do as commanded!

This original form of talisman has pretty much gone by the wayside in modern traditions. Instead, this term is used to describe a creation that is made under auspicious astrological circumstances, with base materials suited to the task at hand. An example of this might be blessing an amethyst crystal at noon and carrying it for clear-headedness. Amethyst is a stone often associated with self-control, and the noon hour shines "light" on any confusion we may have. This combination creates talismanic virtue.

Finally, we come to the word *fetish,* and unlike modern vernacular might indicate, in Portuguese *feitico* means "spell." Fetishes seem to have a slightly broader definition than the other items listed here. Quite simply, they are objects that represent power, especially Divine. For example, a statue of Mary is a kind of fetish for many people (and neatly represents the goddess, too). Similarly, but on a more mundane level, a policeman's badge could be considered a kind of fetish as it instills a sense of respect.

With this in mind, a fetish can be anything that inspires strong emotion in you. Combine this emotional response and connection with a little magic and the possibilities become quite amazing. The only thing to bear in mind is that when you look at and use that item in a magical setting, you have to disengage from its more mundane presence. Now you must see it for its spiritual potential.

Some people find it difficult to look at a lamp, for instance, and think of it as remotely magical. When that happens, they cannot use that object for a fetish or any other form of magic, because the metaphysical application just isn't clear. Without that clarity in one's own mind, any object might as well be an imaginary rock, lifeless and wholly confined. I'm sharing this with you because the rule of meaningfulness will become very important as you read this material. If you look at my suggestions for a charm, amulet, talisman, or fetish and they just don't work for you, then by all means, change them!

Processes for Portable Magic

Just as there were various forms of spellcraft, there are also forms to periapt creation. Because I wholly believe that an adept metaphysician knows how to create or adapt their own spells, charms, and rituals, I'm going to take a moment to share some of those forms with you. This way, you can refer back to them when you'd like to try fashioning something wholly of your own devising.

Charms

As mentioned earlier, charms can be created from objects, words, or symbols. If a charm is created from an object, most practitioners cleanse, bless, and charge that object in some manner. Cleansing is simply a way of getting rid of residual energy that might taint your magic, for example, dipping the object in saltwater. Blessing sets aside that object for a specific function, then charging it saturates the object with the desired energy akin to a battery.

(By the way, old batteries make really neat charms for overall energy!)

One of the most common ways to charge an object is to add a verbal charm to the equation, because that is the original form of charms anyway. This maintains a continuity of form, function, and process. It also instills the will of the practitioner in that item by saturating it with the vibrations of the spoken word.

If a charm is designed to be verbal, it is customary to repeat the charm a certain number of times, sometimes over a set number of days, weeks, or months. However, the verbal charm initially is recited when it's needed. The remaining repetitions are meant to support that original moment both simply by the action of repeating the phrase, and by the number of times it's repeated.

Written or symbolic charms often bear a shape that has meaning to the overall goal. The color chosen for that representation and even the type of medium on which the words or symbols get placed can all increase the metaphorical value. This type of charm is often carried, and it can have an activating word or phrase that turns on the energy.

Why bother with the activating word? By using one, you're helping to stretch the energy in the charm; in other words, it will last longer before you have to re-empower it. The downside of this is that under emergency circumstances, there isn't always time to fire off a phrase to get your magic moving!

As an elementary form of magic, charms need not be contrived in a sacred space. As with spells, they certainly benefit from one, but it's not a requirement of this particular type of periapt.

Amulets

Most ancient amulets were contrived from semi-precious stones (often carved), metals, and plant parts mingled together and kept with a person. If you review the old texts, the process of putting these items together was incredibly specific. The base material, the way it was put together, and the timing of the creation all had to be perfect for the amulet to work properly. I suspect the early mages went to such extents because they felt that protecting one's health, wealth, and position was worthy of a little extra effort!

Another interesting thing noted in early texts was that the order of crafting had symbolic value. For example, if you were making an amulet that protected a relationship, it would need to contain two items (for the couple), to which various symbols might be carved in a specific sequence. In this case, a heart for love, followed by the rune of the warrior, which looks like an upward pointing arrow, and the rune of protection might be used. The love is the foundation that gives the magic its cohesiveness. The warrior then stands between the love and that which is threatening the love. Then at the outer edges of this item, the protection rune represents the whole purpose, providing the finishing touches.

That having been said, certain stones and objects have long been considered as having amuletic qualities without all this fuss. In Persia, turquoise was said to protect a person when travelling, for example, and a branch of coral turns the evil eye in some European countries. So, although the process became important to amuletic creation as history wore on, originally it seems that our ancestors trusted nature's unadorned powers. This means that you can measure both outlooks against your heart and determine which approach makes the most sense and has the most meaning to you.

Talismans

As amulets became more complex in their fashioning, talismans followed suit. In most texts, talismans were described in great detail, from the base material to incantations and auspicious timing. Now, when one considers that originally this process was contrived to please an indwelling spirit who might have to live there for a very long time, the complexity seems to have merit. After all, I'm not sure I'd want my house just slapped together either!

Additionally, if the base material didn't suit the spirit, there could be harmful effects to that spirit when the mage tried to pour that essence into the object. Think of what happens when two discordant vibrations hit one another. That's the same effect that occurs when talismans aren't made properly.

That having been said, because the talismans described herein won't be employing summoned spirits, you can use the pattern provided by history as a guideline instead of an edict. I do recommend choosing the time for making such items carefully, because this generally improves the overall results. I also strongly believe that for a talisman to function properly, the base material needs to vibrationally match the talisman's functions. In the construct of a sacred space, a symbol is no less powerful than that which it represents. In fact, one becomes the other!

Fetishes
Because fetishes were highly tribal in nature, it's hard to find any sort of continuity in how people made them. The process varied from one culture to another, and even sometimes from one house to another! So, how do you choose your materials for fetishes and know they'll work properly? Good question, and one to which I'm giving an educated opinion.

From what I can tell, most fetishes were derived from natural materials. A bit of the plant or animal spirit was believed to still reside in those materials and empower them, thus fulfilling the external power requirement mentioned previously. So, if a plant or animal part comes into your hands and you feel a special energy there, that would be a good start. I also think that man-made objects can bear energy signatures of great worth and power, so don't overlook that option either.

It also seems that fetishes were worn when needed for protection, burned when instant manifestation was desired, scattered to spread energy over an area or group, or thrown away for banishing. This tells us that fetishes served both long and short-term goals.

Worn fetishes were made sturdy and often included reflective objects to turn away negativity. Disposable fetishes were made with Earth-friendly items in the appropriate size and condition to work in whatever medium (Fire, Water, Air, and so forth) the Shaman had in mind. We should remember these kinds of considerations when making our own, but beyond that, the actual logistics are up to each individual.

Charm, Amulet, Talisman, and Fetish Basics
Realistically, everything I told you about spellcraft applies to portable magic, too. The only difference here is that you want to have something easily carried (without spilling or damaging)

and saturated with positive energy when you're done. You can help with the easily carried part by picking small, durable, symbolic foundations. I've used many of the items on the following list as a charm or part of one:

- Seeds
- Buttons
- Crystals/stones
- Leaves
- Spices
- Paperclips
- Business cards
- Nuts/bolts
- Pens/pencils
- Toys
- Compacts
- Jewelry
- Candles
- Stamps
- Paper
- Cloth
- Matches
- Small tools
- Baby wipes
- Envelopes
- Lottery tickets
- Memory chips
- Sewing kits
- Guitar picks
- Storage containers
- Dry beans
- Batteries
- Flowers
- Pins
- Ribbons
- Mirrors
- Bells
- Coupons
- Foils
- Keys
- Lipstick
- Toothpicks
- Coins
- Rice

This is a very abbreviated list, but it gives you a good idea of how many things are compact, durable, and filled with magical potential. Don't limit your imagination; think out of the box! The world around is filled with all kinds of natural and man-made wonders, all of which can be applied creatively in periapt creation if we approach them respectfully.

What about money magic specifically? Well, exactly how you apply the base item in your portable magic depends not only on its mundane use and symbolism, but also how you think about that item. Storage containers might be a good place to put your stock reports to preserve your investment. Coupons might be dabbed with mint oil before shopping to attract bargains your way. The memory chip can be anointed with rosemary, so you remember not to go over your budget.

Cash Charms, Abundance Amulets, Financial Fetishes, and Treasure Talismans

Move Up in the World
You can immediately take a newborn up a flight of stairs upon arriving home to insure their upward movement in society. To apply this symbolism to an adult charm, simply add a verbal component every time you go up a set of stairs or even an elevator. One example might be:

> *"As I climb this set of stairs,*
> *Lift my worries, lift my cares.*
> *No troubles with money, no competitor vies;*
> *From now on, I'm on the rise!"*

Security Stones
Our ancestors often wore or carried various stones, frequently in the form of jewelry, to improve their financial fates. In particular, carry pyrite if you want the foresight to use your money wisely, cat's-eye to keep whatever resources you have at your disposal safe, coal so your money increases, and jade for success in a pressing business deal.

Give to Receive
In keeping with the idea of security stones, give someone a gift of jade, particularly a bracelet or necklace, so they will prosper. Karmically, this will likewise attract blessings to you!

Coin a Phrase

Take four coins minted in the year of your birth and place them in a pouch with a magnet on the next waxing to full moon cycle. Carry it with you regularly after this to attract money. If you don't have a magnet, stitch these into new items of clothing so fortune favors you.

If you can't find coins but have a magnet, draw a dollar sign in green marker and put this on the refrigerator underneath the magnet so money "sticks" where it belongs.

Seed Money

Put a few alfalfa seeds in your wallet or purse. These protect your resources and safeguard you from adversity. An alternative to alfalfa is sesame. In this case, I suggest saying "open sesame" when you place the seeds where desired to open the way toward wealth.

All Purpose Fortune Charm

There are several items that have been used for a very long time as good luck and fortune charms. Why not combine them together for more power and symbolic value? A four-leaf clover, a sliver of cedar wood, a five-petaled lilac, a bit of moss from a gravestone, and a circle of string will all fit easily into a small carrying container. As you put them inside, you might want to add a verbal charm to unify the energies. Here's one example:

"A leaf parted in four from which blessings shall pour;
From cedar wood, reap fortunes for good;
Money from moss, suffer no loss;
Flower petals—five, the magic's alive;
Circle and string, abundance bring!"

Norse Money Charm

The Norse Pagans used an emblem, called the Fehu rune, to encourage prosperity and providence. When you draw it on paper, you're supposed to write *"my need is great"* just beneath it. Carry this paper until your wish manifests, then burn it with a prayer of thanks.

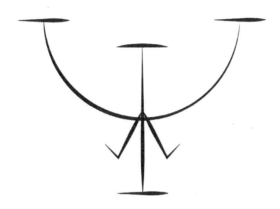

Norse Money Charm

Out of the Horse's Mouth?

Actually, it's more accurate to say "the horse's foot!" It's still common today to see horseshoe charms in homes. Hang them open end up to "catch" luck, or open end down to pour out abundance.

Something Fishy

It was very common during the Victorian era to wear a charm shaped like, or containing the image of, a fish when trying to attract wealth. Usually this was a piece of jewelry, but other options include a tie, scarf, T-shirt, and even socks!

The Buzz

Another Victorian charm is that of a bee. This one attracts business success through its associations with hard work and prosperity. Additionally, if you want to improve your communication skills for important meetings and negotiations, eat a little honey before you leave. That way both the bee and the fruit of its labors can combine for victory. Honey is also said to inspire the muse!

Lucky Leaf

Pluck an ash leaf that has an even number of divisions while wishing for prosperity. Keep this with you until it crumbles, then release it to a wind fluttering toward you so it can blow improvements your way.

For overall luck, add this incantation to the equation when you pick the leaf:

> *"Ash of leaf, I do thee pluck,*
> *To bring to me a year of luck!"*

When the Mountain Won't Come...

I like to inscribe the following emblem, which looks like three upside-down Us or mountains, when I want to overcome adversity. In this case, because you're trying to overcome financial woes, use an indelible marker or pen on a piece of cloth, which lasts longer than paper, and keep it with your money.

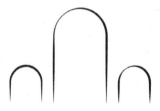

Not So Corny

Keeping dried corn kernels or even popcorn in your home is a way to encourage prosperity. Sprinkle them around your property to protect what you value, and place small sachets of kernels inside piggy banks or near the area where you pay bills or track your finances. This tradition comes from America in the Victorian period.

Wear It?
Colors can become charms and amulets too, simply choosing your clothing wisely. Wear green for financial growth, orange to gather in the harvest of hard labors, or black when you need to be "in the black"!

At the Threshold of Prosperity
A very simple charm that was used in several parts of the world to attract money is that of a silver coin buried under your doorstep or affixed to the back of your doormat. It should be an actual silver coin (not simply silver-toned) for best results, and if it's a coin received for work you've done, all the better.

To give this charm more power, add a verbal element:

"When money comes through my door,
Multiply it by two, then four.
Where'er there's want, let blessings pour;
More is less, and less is more!"

Key to Wisdom
The ancient Greeks often carried special keys to represent power. It's a helpful attribute when accumulating and managing finances, so why not give it a try? Find an old key that's easily recognizable on your key chain and bless it, saying:

"Janus, the gatekeeper, forward and back you see;
Help me manage my finances with this key!"

Note: Janus is a Greek god who had two heads, one facing the future and one the past.

Rune Riches

In Norse tradition, runes were far more than simply divinatory devices. Each symbol was said to evoke power, and for a long time they were a kind of language unto themselves. If you carve or write any of the symbols on the following page, they can become a charm for specific goals.

By the way, you can combine these rune meanings with a color to give your charm more power and symbolic value. For example, building foundations might be drawn in brown because it's the color of soil. Progress that results from hard work might be drawn in orange, the color of the harvest.

Trouble in the Wind

In making your charms, amulets, talismans, and fetishes for success with a loan, it's highly recommended that you avoid the days of March 31 and April 1. In some traditions, borrowing at this time results in disaster, and thus the energies aren't right for making such periapts.

Daylight Savings Time

When the clock turns back an hour, use it wisely! Take that hour and devote yourself to monetary projects, such as clipping coupons or reading over potential investments. In this case, by doing so you're using the symbolism of savings and the bonus hour to empower yourself as a charm!

It's in the Stars

If you see a shooting star in the sky, say the simple verbal charm "money" three times before it goes out of sight. This will attract improved finances in the days ahead, often within three days.

Completing tasks, finalizing financial papers

Overall prosperity

New projects, starting from scratch

Using energy and resources wisely

Progress resulting from hard work

Success, overcoming the odds

Building solid foundations

Talisman of Finding

Take a sprig of goldenrod in hand and walk with it outstretched. Observe carefully as you go. When it bends down, there treasure lies! Alternatives to goldenrod include a pomegranate branch and snakeroot, which specifically locates money.

It's a Bet!

A tradition among the Romani people claims that sprinkling a lottery or horse ticket with nutmeg within twenty-four hours of the event makes it a sure winner. Because I'm not a great advocate of using games of chance to further fortunes, consider applying this idea to job interviews and important business meetings by sprinkling yourself with a little nutmeg to improve your chances of success.

Breaking the Engagement

It was once the custom to break a glass or plate when a couple got engaged to insure their future fortune. I suspect the symbolism here came from sympathetic magic (that is, the glass or plate was broken, but not the power of love). Because our goal is a little more frugal in nature, just eat off paper plates at an engagement instead and toss them away rather than breaking a perfectly good dish!

Laying a Web

When you're trying to recoup valuable items that were lost, or retrieve misappropriated monies, wear the image of a spider. It will trap the right magic in a web, so the items or money goes no further until you find it again.

Wheat Wealthy

In some parts of England, the final sprig of wheat gathered and blessed in the fall was meant to stay in one's home until the following fall to ensure abundance of harvest the next season. It acts as a household talisman for providence and wealth. If you live in an urban area, put some grain bread or cereal in a storage container that's left undisturbed instead.

Lucrative Lunar Energy

If you're going to make a charm or amulet to bless and protect a financial transaction, always do so on the first day following a new moon. This improves the power and luck in the charm.

Marrying into Money

During a wedding, one partner (typically the groom) should carry three grains of salt and three coins in their left pocket. The other (typically the bride) carries a coin in their shoe. This guarantees the couple's prosperity.

Pebble Power

Take a walk in a place with a lot of small stones that you can look through. Try to find one that appears a bit like a kidney bean in shape. According to folklore, this is a natural charm for increasing one's fortune.

The Hearth of the Matter

In Italian homes, it is customary to keep a garlic braid near the hearth to avert poverty, as well as evil and negative energies. This braid can be used for cooking but should always maintain one head of garlic so that the magic stays intact.

If you want, you can add a verbal charm when you put the braid up:

> *"In this sacred garlic braid,*
> *My security is tied, my future staid."*

Sage Advice

An old bit of herblore says that if you find a sage plant bearing a leaf with one black spot on it, you can uproot it to find treasure. Rather than going that far, I'd suggest just picking the leaf and using it as part of money incense, or placing it in your wallet, where a small treasure lies.

It's good to add an incantation when you pick the leaf to designate it for your intention. Here's one example for when you're trying to get a raise:

"Leaf of wise and ancient sages,
Help me to improve my wages!"

Bread Bounty
Bread is considered an excellent symbol of providence in numerous lands. Giving it to a newly married couple acts as a charm so they will never want. Similarly, you can keep breadcrumbs in your house for ongoing sustenance, sprinkling out a pinch to the birds when you have a great need that must be met quickly.

Pumpkin Talisman
In several cultures, pumpkin seeds are said to be wealth talismans. Dry some from your Halloween pumpkin carving, which already has energy for protection, and string them. Remove one and release it to a live water source running toward you when you need to manifest money quickly. For slow, steady financial growth, plant one in rich soil.

Mirror Magic
Mirrors can reflect negativity or direct energy in other ways depending on how you place them. As a protective amulet, turn mirrors outward, especially in the area where you keep your money, such as a safe. As you do this, say:

"Poverty and troubles, away, away,
Only good fortune may stay!"

To attract bounty, use the mirror as a charm and draw a dollar sign on it, then turn the mirror toward your money, saying:

"Mirror magic turned within,
So my spellcraft can begin.
Attract good fortune and money my way,
As long as here this mirror stays!"

June Bonus

June is a propitious month for making money charms. In particular, blessing an agate with black-and-white veins and carrying it during this month is said to fight adversity. Try adding a verbal component to this timing:

"Bounty and blessing in this stone are stored;
Attract to me financial rewards!"

Iron It Out

Take a hazel stick and cap it with iron at both ends. This creates a type of dousing rod. When you carry it with you, it helps uncover gold. Bear in mind, however, that the gold can be figurative, such as a gold-colored piece of clothing that's on sale!

Fern Fortunes

Find a bit of male fern and dry a frond. In ancient spell books, this is called a "lucky hand," and it's a natural charm for good fortune. If kept near your money, it will attract that luck specifically to where you need it most! To improve the effect, however, add a verbal element:

"Hand of fortune, hand of luck,
Grant this boon, help me save some bucks!"

I should warn you that the universe has a sense of humor, so if you happen to be driving down a road and nearly miss a deer, don't be overly surprised. Indirectly, however, this also just saved you a fortune in car repairs!

Lemon Luxury

To make yourself into a walking money charm for a full day, bathe before you go out in warm water where lemon verbena has been steeped. The energy of this herb will saturate your aura and help you bring home a steady flow of money. Remember when you're out during the day to watch for opportunity to present itself; for instance, if something seems like an odd coincidence, look more closely! This charm only lasts one day, but it can be refreshed with a new bath.

Dock Dollars

Carry yellow dock seeds or scatter them to the winds to encourage prosperity. Alternatively, create a dollar sign with glue on green paper and sprinkle the seeds on top so your money will stick to you like glue!

Sun Tea Talisman

On the first day of spring, or at dawn on any day, treat yourself to some Sun tea. The Sun is a symbol of blessing and prosperous, growth-oriented energy. To accomplish this, simply let the water bask in the Sun's rays, with the tea bag steeping therein. When it's strong enough for your tastes, add a slice of lemon to clarify your purpose and say:

> *"Blessed by the Sun,*
> *The magic's begun;*
> *When taken to lips,*
> *Blessings in each sip."*

Drink the tea, allowing the talisman to energize you for that day. (This is another one-day item.)

By the way, you can change the type of tea you make to better reflect your goals, which is also an appropriate way to make a talisman. For example, mint tea is associated with increasing money, whereas chamomile safeguards what you have, giving you peace of mind.

Woodruff Whimsy

Woodruff flowers are a natural fetish that, when carried, bring a change in your finances. You need to specify the type of change you want! In this case, you might tuck them in a pocket, saying:

> *"Turn and change, my finances rearrange,*
> *So bills get paid. Here magic's laid;*
> *Let my prosperity never fade."*

Abracadabra

The Chaldeans used the word *abracadabra*, written in the form of an upside-down triangle, to banish sickness. Drawing on this idea, get a piece of paper and inscribe on it a symbol that to you represents abundance. Over this symbol write a stylized word or phrase that designates the area of your life where you need that abundance most. Begin with one letter of that word or phrase, moving downward on the paper, until you have the complete wish at the bottom as shown here:

a
abu
abund
abundan
abundance
abundance f
abundance fro
abundance from w
abundance from wri
abundance from writing

Tin Talisman

Tin is a very soft metal. Find a small square and wrap it around an amethyst crystal and a piece of paper bearing the symbol of Jupiter on it (see the following illustration).

Jupiter

This should be done on a Thursday. If you can create the talisman during the first or eighth hour of the day, or third or tenth hour of the night, all the better. As you wrap the tin, say:

> *"Crystal wrapped in tin, let the magic begin
> On this propitious day, let prosperity have its way."*
> *Carry this with you to manifest the energy.*

Hex It!

The Pennsylvania Dutch often painted special images called *hex signs* on their houses; some believe it is to protect their treasured possessions, especially the land and the people living thereon. Two of those images are more correlated with plenty and abundance than others. If you know a leather tooler or a painter, you might want to have one of the signs on the following page re-created on your wallet, your front door, or your place of business.

Hair Affair

In certain cultures, hair was valuable enough to use as money. Keeping one's hair long creates a living prosperity and strength charm. However, because many of us don't want to wear our hair long, instead I recommend saving some strands and snippets to use a part of your money charms. This is a piece of you, so it creates an energy signature and imprint to personalize the magic.

Horn of Plenty

Keep a horn of plenty in your home; one made of straw or another harvest product is better than a pottery one. Toss your pocket change into it daily, so the money flows back out of the opening. Symbolically, this helps the course of prosperity. I do, however, recommend giving this change to good causes so that karmically you'll be thrice blessed!

Golden Grasshopper

The image of a grasshopper painted gold, or one kept as a pet, evokes wealth. Grasshoppers are very easy to keep as pets, but for the magic to be maintained, you need to care for it well—as you would want your money cared for!

Tenacious Turtle

Find an old tortoiseshell comb and weave a dollar bill into it. Keep this in a safe place to increase your finances, along with your tenacity for keeping track of same! To improve the overall power in this charm, wrap it in red flannel. Red is a power color that keeps evil or negative intent away from that which you're safeguarding.

Sunny Side Talisman

Take a yellow piece of paper and draw a Sun on it. During the eighth hour of the day, the third hour of the night, or the tenth hour of the night, wrap this around a piece of amber (a squarish piece if you can find one, to accent foundations), saying:

> *"Wrapped herein, wealth and riches,*
> *Keep away financial glitches!"*

Coral Consciousness

As I mentioned earlier, coral has been used as currency for thousands of years. Some people would even tie a piece of coral found at the beach to any item they wished to make fruitful (people, trees, animals, and money). Using this idea, attach a piece to your debit card or wallet. If the coral ever breaks, you must replace the charm because that also breaks the natural magic therein.

By the way, businesspeople can apply this on a slightly larger scale by putting pieces in a cash drawer or register along with a piece of kelp. The kelp attracts more clients!

Bounty Beans

Find or make a small green pouch. Place therein one vanilla bean and one tonka bean, saying:

> *"Abundance and wealth come in many forms.*
> *From this charm, love and money be born!"*

When carried regularly, these two beans work together to manifest improved finances and stronger loving relationships .

Flying the Flag of Success

Tibetan prayer flags are much more common to see in New Age stores and college dorm rooms than they used to be, but they still attract prosperity, happiness, and victories when they are created and flown correctly. If you'd like to make a version of these charmed flags yourself, it requires you to paint the writings from a sacred text of your choice, a goldfish, an umbrella (Sun wheel), a vase, a sign for victory, a conch shell, a good luck diagram, a lotus flower, and a wheel onto small cloth squares. Two goldfish is a particularly prosperous image on these flags, though they can have any sort of deity, mantra, or other symbol you associate with abundance. You can style these in any manner that has meaning to you (preferably in weather-resistant paint), then hoist the flag for success!

Propagating Change
When someone gives you change, rather than spend it, put it in a new purse or wallet. This protects that item against ever being empty again.

Jaded
Whenever you need to make important financial choices, rub a piece of jade. This will help guide you toward the decision that will bring the greatest amount of success and profit.

As you can see, charms, amulets, talismans, and fetishes can be incredibly simple or complex, depending on your personal feelings on the matter. However, all of them might benefit from the use of rituals to empower and bless them.

Chapter Six

RICH RITUAL

"Ritual is the way you carry the presence of the sacred. Ritual is the spark that must not go out."
—Christina Baldwin

For those times when you want a more formal atmosphere in which to weave magic for "enrichment," the ritual space is a perfect choice. But to do so you must first have a grasp of the whys and how-tos of this process. For many of us, the word ritual engenders memories of long Sunday sermons and fidgeting in a pew. Magic need not be like that. In fact, ritual as a life-affirming process has the potential of being anything but boring or tedious. The key to success here is threefold: an intimate understanding of ritual, sound planning, and meaningfulness.

Understanding Ritual and Its Purpose

Beginning with comprehension, ritual is a way of expressing outwardly what's happening in our inner life. It is also a way of acknowledging what's happening all around us in various situations, to other people, and on the Earth as a whole. Finally, and perhaps most importantly, ritual is a vehicle for keeping us connected with Spirit and the ebb and flow of magical energy in all things.

Although this may sound daunting, you really enact rituals every day already. You have patterns that you follow in your routine that provide continuity and familiarity. When you don't follow that pattern or miss part of it, something seems amiss all day. If you don't believe me, watch what happens when someone forgets a power tie for a special meeting or can't find a favorite coffee mug!

Magical ritual is a lot like that. It's a pattern of words and actions followed on a regular basis to keep spiritual energy alive and well in your life. This, in turn, provides comfort, enables an awareness of cycles, increases joy, and improves overall harmony within and without.

What sets magical ritual apart from our everyday rituals is intention. Each ritual has a focus or goal associated with it. That focus or goal may be honoring a season, commemorating a special occasion, understanding a spiritual lesson more fully, or simply celebrating fellowship; whatever the goal, it's something around which the entire ritual revolves. From planning to completion, that intention is built in word and deed on a mundane, mental, and spiritual level, effectively creating a three-dimensional pattern for the resulting magic to follow.

With this in mind, it's easy to see why the manifesting power in a properly enacted ritual could be quite astounding. On the other hand, there is little worse to wade through than a really bad ritual. The information here will hopefully help you avoid the latter.

Ritual Components and Processes

As with all other parts of magic, rituals have components and processes to follow. These might change slightly from tradition to tradition, and ritual to ritual, to illustrate that tradition's or ritual's uniqueness. Nonetheless, there are many commonalities that we can focus on and consider in our own ritual creation.

The Components

In order to give sensual form to a ritual, most include some type of components, each of which is chosen and blessed for its symbolic value. Among these we might find the traditional tools of many Wiccans, such as candles, a goblet, incense, and an athame (ritual dagger). We also might find wine, water, or milk as a libation; token offerings to the Divine; and various decorations that augment the theme (for example, a pumpkin at Samhain or flowers at Spring Equinox).

In addition to this, some of the things that might be included in a ritual are:

- **Music:** Sometimes played in the background or added as part of a meditation or circle dance.
- **Robes or Costumes:** To help put people in the right frame of mind (metaphysical instead of mundane).
- **Symbolic Timing:** Some rituals must, by their nature, take place on or near a set date (such as our seasonal and lunar observances). Others can be timed for propitious astrological moments if a practitioner so chooses. To accomplish this, it helps to have a good astrological calendar to which to refer to for Moon signs and phases.
- **Invocations:** Welcome guardian energy and help in creating the sacred space. Many invocations start in the East and end in the North. Some type of similar wording is used at the end of a ritual, dismissing those powers with gratitude while moving counterclockwise to dismantle the energy.
- **Prayers and Meditations:** Connect us with the Sacred, settle one's spirit, and improve spiritual awareness. Only some rituals include one, the other, or all of these; it depends on the occasion.

- ◆ **Spellcraft and Other Magical Methods:** Very frequently, practitioners will take advantage of the protection and improved energies of a sacred space for spellcasting, periapt creation, and other techniques.
- ◆ **Dance and Chanting:** Two very effective ways to raise power, the first through physical movement, which generates energy, and the second through verbal expression, which puts sympathetic vibrations into the air. These two methods were very common among various mystical traditions to help people achieve altered states of awareness, too!

Now, although not all rituals include all of these components, you'll find an assortment of each within most rituals you attend or observe. The most important part is finding a combination that works for you and makes sense considering the participants and your goal.

Ritual Processes

Once you have this list of components from which to fashion your own ritual, the next logical step is understanding what constitutes a dependable ritual construct. For the purpose of the material shared here, I'm relying on common methods from Wicca as a foundation. However, various traditions do have other ways of assembling successful ritual that are no less fulfilling or powerful.

Step one to devising a good ritual is setting the mood. This includes the way the room is set up, what sounds and sights people encounter, lighting, and aromatics. Bear in mind that magic takes place out of space and out of time. A well-thought-out ambiance puts everyone in the right frame of mind for all that's to come.

Building on this foundation, it's very important to have all the tools and components for your ritual gathered and placed correctly in the sacred space, so you don't have to stop mid-ritual to hunt for something. Similarly, remember that forewarned is forearmed. If you're working outdoors, don't forget to check the safety of the region, such as watching for roots and stones that could trip participants. Although this sounds rather mundane, the rule of "safety first" doesn't stop when magic starts. If anything, we should be more responsible for ourselves and others in the setting of a sacred space.

You need to make sure that you and/or your participants are all properly prepared for this ritual. For example, do you want to have a ritual bath or meditate beforehand? Do you have a way of clearing people of negativity when they enter the site? Have you asked people to be well rested and to know their parts for the ritual? (In my opinion, there's little worse than poorly recited ritual working from a piece of paper.)

If there is a theme to the ritual that you want people to accentuate with decorations for the altar or their clothing, let them know well ahead of time! Also, bring some backups for those who inevitably forget. Children in particular love to pick out items to help deck the sacred space; it's important to include our future generations in our magic when the ritual's theme allows.

Once everyone gathers, take a moment or two to get in sync with each other. Unified breathing is one way to accomplish this task, as is a brief meditation. Try inhaling on the count of three, holding it for a three count, and exhaling on a three count. Repeat this five to ten times until you sense a settling of mind and spirit. Bear in mind, this is well worth the time. If everyone present isn't aware and in tune with each other's energy, the ritual will not go as well as it might.

Lastly comes the creation of sacred space. Now, every group I've encountered has different invocations to call the guardians and Spirit, and every person I know has an opinion as to how formal or informal a sacred space should be. To my thinking, if time is short or needs are pressing, an informal sacred space is fine.

How do I define an informal sacred space? This would be an area in which symbolic items were charged and placed in the four quarters before the event. Typically, these items have symbolic value to their placement, such as a candle in the South for Fire, and a feather in the East for Air.

Come the actual ritual, a very short invocation would serve to activate these items that already resonate with sacred energies. My favorite example of this is my invocation:

"Earth, Air, Fire, and Sea, I call you all, come dance with me!"

Although you'd have to adjust this for a group, you've accomplished in one sentence what can take upward of twenty minutes in a more formalized setting.

When time allows, a more formal calling is nice. It gives each person time to adjust to the elemental energies being called forth, and to the diversity of energies present. In turn, it will also create a more astrally solid field of protective energy than the quickie approach described previously.

The more formal calling of the quarters often begins in the East (the region of dawn), then proceeds around the circle clockwise with a final prayer or invocation at the center. The only time the calling is done counterclockwise is when the sacred space is being prepared for a banishing or negating of some type of energy or situation. I have seen rituals where the invocation begins at another quarter, however. For example, on Earth Day a ritual for Earth healing might begin in the North quarter, which is associated with the Earth element.

Typically, the calling of the quarters is addressed to the element or direction (Earth, Air, Fire, Water or North, East, South and West, respectively). A minor variation I've seen on this is calling upon four gods or goddesses (or a mixture) from the same cultural tradition to watch over the sacred space. The only problem here becomes making sure all these powers will work effectively together; Divine beings can become rather jealous.

As each quarter is invoked, something usually takes place in that region of the circle to honor the energy. When invoking Air, incense might be ignited, for example, or when invoking Water, some liquid might be sprinkled or poured out.

Other Potential Symbols for the Elements

- **Earth:** Soil, potted plant, seeds, globe, brown or green colored items.
- **Air:** Fan, open window, wind chimes, bird imagery, yellow and other pastel colors.
- **Fire:** Brazier, light source, representation of the Sun, red—or orange—colored items.
- **Water:** Seashells, driftwood, bowl, silver—or blue—colored items.

This process honors the element and provides a visual cue to participants that increases the symbolic value of what's occurring.

Sample Invocation

Air/East:

"I stand at dawn,
Here, a strand of purple light,
Kisses the horizon with hope;
All of nature stirs,
And creation's breath whispers 'cross,

A world filled with potential.
Come! Winds from the four corners,
Guides and Guardians,
Heed our call.
Wrap your blessed breezes round us gently,
Awaken our minds, inspire our spirits."

Fire/South:

"I stand at noon,
Here, a sphere of golden glory,
Blazes high in the sky with power,
Embracing the vista in warmth;
All of nature sings,
And creation's pulse beats loud and long 'cross,
A world filled with life.
Come! Fires from the four corners,
Guides and Guardians,
Heed our call.
Burn brightly in this sacred space,
To banish the darkness, unite our heartbeat, and,
Rekindle our souls."

Water/West:

"I stand at dusk,
Here, the Sun withdraws to the ancestor's sea,
Glowing orange, pink and blue with acceptance,
Resting its light in the cradle of an ancient wave;
All of nature chants,
Calling the night, reclaiming the night 'cross,
A world filled with wonder.
Come! Waters from the four comers,
Guides and Guardians,
Heed our call.
Wash gently through this sacred space,

Quench our thirst, cleanse us, and make us,
Whole."

Earth/North:

"I stand at midnight,
Here, the Earth waits silent and expectant,
In between breaths and moments, sounds and silences,
In the moonlight, and the shadow of a star;
All of nature pauses,
Between the worlds, all time and none 'cross,
A world filled with magic.
Come! Earth from the four corners,
Guides and Guardians,
Heed our call.
Sprinkle your rich soils beneath our feet,
Plant us firmly on our path,
Make us one."

This invocation could be presented by up to four people. If you decide to use four individuals, the people involved should be keyed into the element they invoke; ask them which element they relate to most strongly and what empowers them to determine this. Afterward, a prayer or invocation to Spirit often follows. Which face of the god or goddess is called upon depends on the path involved. I simply prefer to refer to the god/dess as the Sacred Parent, Source, or Spirit, figuratively covering all bases!

Sample Prayer to Spirit

"Great Spirit, you who have always been and shall always be,
I bid you welcome. Please join us in this sacred space as we
celebrate (occasion),

And focus our energy on (your overall goal—that is, where you're
sending the energy you raise).
Let your blessings flow from hand to hand and heart to heart,
As we meet in perfect trust and love.
Help us honor our magic, and our place in the Circle of life.
Help us honor each other, and the specialness that is in
each human being.
And help us honor this moment between the worlds,
Where we weave our spells and come to understand our
part as cocreators.
So be it!"

Once this sacred space is invoked, it remains in place until the end of the ritual. At this juncture, the "body" of the ritual begins: dances, activities, ritual plays, spells, or whatever is on the proverbial magical menu for the event. Each of the activities that take place now is designed to build energy toward the goal or theme of the ritual, and at some point, the person or group will release the power and send it on its way, often just prior to dismissing the sacred space.

Finally, the circle is closed, usually working counterclockwise for dismissal and thanks to the guardians. Many rituals are followed by a small feast or munchies, along with hearty amounts of fellowship for all who attended. The food helps people to ground after the magic so they're not driving home with their heads in the clouds! It also helps people internalize what has just occurred on a personal level.

If you feel you need a more detailed guide to ritual, I suggest my guide *A Witch's Book of Ceremonies and Rituals* as a starting point. It provides specific information and examples that cannot be provided here due to space.

Using and Adapting Pre-Written Rituals

Before I move forward into the sample rituals, I'd like to digress
for just a moment to talk about pre-written material that's not
of your (or your group's) making. Do not simply enact these
because someone, somewhere said, "Hey, try this!" Read them
over carefully. Look at the wording. Check all the components
and methods presented, then ask yourself:

◆ Are these words I can say comfortably and honestly?
◆ Is the ritual construct meaningful to me, or to everyone
   who plans to participate in the ritual?
◆ Is there anything here that goes against my ethical code
   or personal taboos?
◆ Do the timing and suggested components make sense
   considering the theme of the ritual?
◆ Is there enough material here so that those who would
   like to participate can?

If you find yourself answering no to any of the aforementioned
questions, there are two solutions: Write a ritual from scratch
yourself or adapt the one you have. Redo the words, maintaining
the meaning, with phrases more common to you or your group.
Add little touches throughout the ritual that will help it be more
familiar and significant to participants. Remove anything that goes
against your moral fiber, adding something else more suitable.
Adjust the timing and components so the symbolic value to you
or your group seems more fitting. Finally, if need be, add a few
extra activities so everyone who chooses can be involved.

Why go through all this fuss? Well, you might like the
idea behind a ritual and even a lot of the components but

discover, as a whole, something is lacking. By taking the time to personalize and adjust it, you'll end up with a ritual that will flow more smoothly. It will also be more meaningful, and therefore more effective.

Sample Rituals

Money rituals can have any number of focal points. These examples should have some universal appeal, or a minimally good base of material with which to work.

Generic Attendance and Blessings

At least once a year, it's good to enact a ritual such as this one to encourage the ongoing flow of bounty and blessings in your life. For timing, how about your birthday or an anniversary? This ritual suits both this goal and the suggested timing by adapting a fairly common rite of blessing that works with the chakras, the energy centers of the body.

What You'll Need
- A white candle
- A cup of apple juice placed on your altar or another central location in the ritual room
- Anointing oil (almond oil with cinnamon and ginger is one good choice)
- Note that this ritual is designed for one person but could be adapted to more simply by having people take turns blessing each other rather than doing it yourself.

Calling the Quarters

Begin in the East and move clockwise to the South, West, and North, saying:

> *"The Air is my breath—alive and pure.*
> *The wind is my source and encouragement.*
> *Guardians of the East, be welcome here!*
> *Protect this space and bless me with your motivation.*
> *The Fire is my blood—warm and vital.*
> *The light is my guide and vision.*
> *Guardians of the South, be welcome here.*
> *Protect this space and bless me with your power.*
> *The Water is my tears—cleansing and healing.*
> *The wave is my momentum and refreshment.*
> *Guardians of the West, be welcome here.*
> *Protect this space and bless me with your inspiration.*
> *The Earth is my body—nourishing and supportive.*
> *The soil is my heritage and grounding.*
> *Guardians of the North, be welcome here and bless me with*
> *your maturity."*

The Body of the Ritual

Next, move to the area where the candle, cup, and oils are situated. Light the candle to welcome Spirit. Take the cup in both hands and hold it up toward the sky, saying:

> *"Great Spirit, your light shines in this sacred space, and in my spirit.*
> *Bless this cup that it may provide me with wisdom in the year ahead,*
> *And grant me the fruitfulness of Earth's abundance."*

Drink the cup completely to accept the blessing. Next, take the oil and put a little on your index finger. Dab this on the top of your head, the space on your forehead between your eyes, your heart, your hands, and your feet (in sequence), saying:

"Bless my mind that I might think clearly about my resources.
Bless my intuition that I might know when to act and when to wait.
Bless my heart that I might always be ready to give and receive the
richness of love.
Bless my hands that they might work diligently and with skill.
Bless my feet that I might walk the path of beauty,
Balancing spiritual matters with mundane life always.
So be it."

When you're done, you might want to take some time meditating or writing in a journal. Then, blow out the candle and say:

"The magic blessings, once spoken, shall never be broken.
Spirit and Guardians, thank you for your presence here and
your blessings.
As I leave this place keep watch over me,
And continue as my guides in life, in spirit, in truth. So be it."

New Job, Raise, or Promotion

A little word of warning about this ritual: Very frequently, the results seem to be that the new job, raise, or promotion requires more work, focus, or dedication than your present one (unless you're being worked to death for little money). This increase may only be temporary to achieve the main goal, but it's a way that the universe keeps us honest. Stop and ask yourself if you're ready to accept the manner in which the Divine answers this request, even if it's not your vision of what should happen!

Additionally, it is one thing to wish to follow your bliss, but in my humble experience, bliss often doesn't pay well unless you're very clever. The grass is often greener on the other side only until you get there. Then, you discover the window you were looking through was tinted! So, the phrase "look before you leap" applies to magic, too!

What You'll Need

- A business card or other small item that represents an immediate supervisor at your current job (the person who oversees raises or advancement), or the business cards collected from recent interviews that seemed to hold promise
- A reflective piece of paper (such as silver wrapping paper or aluminum foil)
- Braided green, white, and blue string
- Red candle (for energy) on your altar

Calling the Quarters

Begin this invocation in the North (the money and security center of the circle) and proceed around clockwise, saying:

"Watchtower of the North, I call and charge you.
Stand alert and bring with you solid ground on which to
build my dreams.
Watchtower of the East, I call and charge you.
Stand alert and bring with you a fair wind by which to set my course.
Watchtower of the South, I call and charge you.
Stand alert and bring with you the light of understanding,
To guide my decisions and efforts.
Watchtower of the West, I call and charge you.
Stand alert and bring with you the waters of transformation,
And inspiration to enliven my soul."

Go to the candle and light it, saying:

"Fire of power, Fire of change, Fire of Spirit, Fire of creation,
Burn bright in this space, in my heart, in my life.
I put my prayers and wishes before you in truthfulness.

*I need (the specifics of your situation. Use words with which
you're comfortable).
So be it."*

Now collect the business cards you've gathered. Enfold them in the reflective paper (shiny side in), then tie with the string, saying:

*"Green for prosperity and growth,
White for protection and Spirit's guidance,
Blue for happiness and inner peace.
Reflect on my request, turn your mind to thoughts of me.
By my will this spell is freed!"*

Carry the bundle with you to the office or to second interviews. The reflective surface of the paper helps the person represented by the card "reflect" on your qualifications and efforts. Just be aware that this highlights everything, both bad and good!

When you're done, close the circle moving counterclockwise from West to North, saying:

*"The Waters retreat but the thirst is quenched.
The Fires dim, but warm me still and burn within.
The winds are calm, yet the Air is fresh and hopeful.
The Earth is still but filled with potential.
Thanks be to All for protection, for providence, for direction.
Farewell!"*

Dreaming for Dollars

Various dream images might signify something about your financial situation or future. You can help inspire those dreams by making your bedroom into a sacred space and adding a few components that improve your chances of receiving spiritual dreams.

What You'll Need
- ◆ A cup of lavender tea
- ◆ Sandalwood incense
- ◆ A bundle of rose petals mingled with marigolds
- ◆ A paper and pen or device with voice-recording capabilities
- ◆ Place the tea next to your bed, the incense in a fire-safe container and location, and the bundle under your pillow. You will also want to keep the paper and pen or voice recording device very close by for when you wake up.

Calling the Quarters
You'll want to do this from under your covers, using your strong hand outstretched like a wand pointing in the appropriate direction as you speak. Begin in the West (Water has a very relaxing characteristic), saying:

"Waters rock me in your gentle arms.
Watch me ever as I sleep, and in my memory my dreams to keep.
Mother Earth, come hold me close, and join me in my bed.
Let nothing but your visions sweet, fill my sleeping head.
Brother Wind, grant gentle, warm breezes
that fill the world with hope.
Grant to me a special dream that I might better cope.
Father Fire, light the way, as through the dreamscape I roam.
Be my guide, my waymark, ongoing and coming home."

Pick up the cup of tea, saying:

"Gentle spirit of sleep and dreams, from here to the stars
and in moonbeams.
Give me a clear vision to understand, guide me with
your gentle hand."

Sip the tea slowly, letting its peaceful energy fill you, then settle into sleep. This sacred space is not disassembled until after you wake up and record your dreams either on paper or the tape recorder.

In the morning, immediately record any impressions or memories you have upon waking, then release the sacred space with a dismissal:

> *"Spirits, Guides, and Guardians all,*
> *Thank you for hearing my soul's call,*
> *But day has dawned upon my heart,*
> *So merry meet, and merry now part!"*

Resource Stretching

Prosperity magic includes efforts aimed at making the resources at your disposal last as long as possible. This also means making those resources work effectively for you. This ritual is designed to support both goals until your proverbial ship comes in!

What You'll Need
- ◆ Your wallet
- ◆ A printed copy of a recent bank statement
- ◆ A rubber band
- ◆ Small glass of grape wine or juice
- ◆ 1 brown candle (for Earth)
- ◆ All of these will need to be readily accessible within the sacred space.

Calling the Quarters
We will begin this invocation in the North again to stress the need for Earth-related energies (sustenance, providence, and so on), then proceed around the circle clockwise. By the way, if you're using this ritual to banish a streak of particularly bad luck that's

left you wanting, you might want to move counterclockwise and adjust the invocation to reflect that goal.

"Earth spirits, who nurture and sustain me, come join me in
this sacred space.
Protect it from all dangers approaching from the North,
And bless it with your supportive energy.
Air spirits, who encourage and inspire me, come join me in
this sacred space.
Protect it from all dangers approaching from the East,
And bless it with your mindful energy.
Fire spirits, who energize and purify me, come join me in
this sacred space.
Protect it from all dangers approaching from the South,
And bless it with your life-affirming energy.
Water spirits, who heal and motivate me, come join me in
this sacred space.
Protect it from all dangers approaching from the West,
And bless it with your thirst-quenching energy."

Move to the center of the space, light the candle, and say:

"Ancient powers, see the need that lays heavy on my heart.
Here before you are the symbols of our world,
In which money is necessary to sustain our very lives.
Help me to use what I have wisely,
So that every cent purchases threefold goods and services.
Help me to be judicious and aware so that balance is maintained."

Pick up the glass of wine:

"Even as the Earth's bounty provides for our needs,
Now I return it to you in thanks for all that you have given thus far."

Pour out the wine; if you're inside, you can wait until after the ritual to take it outside. Next, take the bank statement and the rubber band and hold them in your hands. Fold the bank statement into thirds, as if you were putting it in an envelope, and place the rubber band around it, saying:

> *"Stretch and adapt,*
> *Stretch and adapt,*
> *Put funds to work for me;*
> *Fill in the gaps!"*

The rubber band stresses the symbolic "stretching" of money. Keep this charm stored in your wallet or with important financial papers.

This is a good time to balance your budget or proceed with any other mundane financial chores you may have neglected. When you're done with those activities, you can close the circle with a dismissal:

> *"Spirits who fill this magic place,*
> *Help my budget maintain an even pace.*
> *And as you leave the sacred space,*
> *Grant to me a prosperous base.*
> *So mote it be."*

If you didn't pour out the wine, don't forget to do it now. Never make promises to the universe unless you plan to keep them!

Cash Quick

Although patience is a virtue, and the universe has its own sense of timing, there are moments when we need money quickly for an emergency. This ritual will help, but only if there truly is a need involved, not simply a craving or flight of fancy.

What You'll Need
- A green candle with a dollar sign carved into it near the top of the candle
- Your debit card, because we associate this with getting quick-fix money
- A Bic lighter (yes, the brand is important here)

Calling the Quarters
Because time is of the essence here, I suggest a similarly quick calling. In this instance, it mirrors the overall goal of your ritual:

> *"Come Air, a changing wind blows.*
> *By Fire, my prosperity shows.*
> *Through Water, my money flows.*
> *In Earth, my money grows."*

Go to where you've placed the green candle and light it with the Bic, saying:

> *"With a willful word and a flick of my Bic,*
> *Bring to me money, quick!*
> *(Thing) is what I need to accumulate,*
> *In (time) days, a true turn of fate!"*

Leave the candle to burn until the image of the dollar bill melts away. Focus wholly on your goal while it burns, and if you wish, you can continue to repeat the verbal charm.

Next, pick up your debit card and hold it between your hands, saying:

> *"When I need it, let money be there.*
> *With my finances, Spirit, take care!*

I have a need that cannot wait;
The debts to pay are already late.
This plastic card with prosperity fill,
So I can pay these pending bills!"

Put the card back in your wallet where it can continue to bless all your money. Keep your eyes open for an opportunity or unexpected windfall.

To close the circle, you might simply want to end with a heartfelt prayer that expresses your need again and thanks both Spirit and the Guardians for any help they can provide.

Banishing Poverty and Encouraging Luck

I have always had the sense that poverty is a kind of spirit that hangs around people like a proverbial black cloud. No one should have to live under such a gray, heavy burden. This ritual is designed to turn things around and manifest a little luck to help out while the magic's working its wonders.

What You'll Need
- Any item you regard as lucky
- A small black candle and fire-safe holder where it can burn down completely
- Some saltwater and sage or cedar incense
- A standard-sized white candle
- An item of clothing that bears your lucky color turned inside out, which you should wear into the ritual
- Both candles should be left near the northern quarter of your circle.

Calling the Quarters
Because this is a banishing ritual, you will be moving counterclockwise. Poverty is associated with the Northern quarter (Earth) and often is a manifestation of not living in harmony with that element, so you will begin there.

"Mother Earth, I would to put my life back on the right path.
So today I cultivate, weed, and seed my soul with your presence.
Let your providence and bounty come to me, now in my hour of need.
Sister Waters, I would to ride your waves to a new shore where
opportunity waits.
Today I drink fully of your healing-ease the wounds this time has
left on my soul.
Let your ever-flowing nature gently guide me in my hour of need.
Father Fire, I would to burn away the old, outmoded ways
and begin anew.
Today I warm myself by your side and refill my soul with your power.
Let your light shine on the path ahead, offering promise with each step.
Brother Wind, bring now the breeze of change so the sky may
clear once more.
Today I breath in your motivational airs and refresh my soul
with your insight.
Let your breath be one with mine, even, full, free, and filled with hope."

Return to the Northern point of your circle and light the
black candle, saying:

"This candle represents these dark days.
It is the blackness of a person who has lost their way.
The blackness of despondency and apathy.
The blackness of insufficiency.
By my will, and my magic, I burn it away.
It shall have no more power over me."

Let the candle burn completely down until nothing remains
but wax, and even that should be thrown out after this ritual to
symbolically throw away your bad luck. While it burns you can
bless your lucky charm by taking it in hand and chanting repeatedly:

"Away, away, bad luck away
Only goodness and fortune may stay!"

Let your voice rise naturally as an affirmation of the magic. Continue chanting until the black candle has burned out completely. Put your lucky charm in a pocket; this needs to be with you as much as possible. Then return to the Northern point and set up the white candle on top of the remnants of the black one; the power of light over darkness is the symbolism here. Say:

"Spirit is the light that casts no shadow.
It is the light of hope, of help, and renewal,
And it shines in my life.
I welcome Spirit. I welcome hope.
I welcome financial renewal.
So mote it be."

This candle may be blown out and saved for other emergency financial rituals or spells.

To close the circle, you will want to walk clockwise to claim your new blessings and accept them. Starting in the East, say:

"The winds bless me with smooth sailing.
The fiery Sun will shine in the sky.
The waters will be gentle and filled with bounty.
The Earth will sing and grant providence,
And I will be thankful. So be it."

It takes a while to get comfortable with ritual and to find yourself adept with it, so please be patient. Many of us aren't used to being our own ministers, but in both money matters and life as a whole that is the goal of our magic.

Chapter Seven

ASTRO CASH AND
FENG SHUI FORTUNE

*"...like the seafaring man on the desert of waters, you choose them as
your guides, and following them you will reach your destiny."*
—Carl Schurz

As the saying goes, there is more than one way to skin a cat. In
this case, however, we're actually putting the proverbial skin
back on by adding the knowledge and methods of astrology and
feng shui to the other techniques already examined in this book.

The obvious question is why mix and match methods? For
one thing, I believe people should have numerous possibilities
from which to choose so that they can find a blend that really
sings with the song of their souls. For another, I feel a truly
adept metaphysician should be educated in many methods and
ideologies, especially those with a proven track record. This
rounds out our world vision and gives our path greater depth.
In turn, our magic has greater dimension and we, as human
beings, have greater respect for the wonders diversity offers.

A third question many readers might ask is what it is about
astrology or feng shui that gives them a special place in this
book. You'll find most of that answer in the information shared

here, but in brief, both are ancient traditions with thousands of years of practical experience to guide us in our modern usage. Astrology in particular manifested in numerous cultural settings giving it a somewhat universal appeal. Meanwhile, feng shui helps us bring East and West together for global thinking, living, and, of course, magic!

Astrology

Astrology as a form of natural omen interpretation began in the ancient past. The first set of cuneiform horoscopes show up around 1800 BCE in Mesopotamia, which come with philosophical and astronomical notes as well, and similar horoscopes sprung in India around 1400 BCE. This amazing history means that modern practitioners have nearly four thousand years of information at their fingertips when working with astrology alone or combined with other techniques.

Now, only a handful of us have the time to sort through four thousand years of information! So, I have focused on the aspects of astrology that can help you with your money magic. The first way is to understand how your birth sign may affect your finances.

The following chart provides an overview of general tendencies with money in each birth sign. Be aware as you read this, though, that astrology is a very complex art and interpretations can change according to your birth hour, the planets in your chart, and so on. Thus, I've provided a very broad generalization that could be better honed by having a professional do a complete chart for you.

Birth Signs and Financial Matters
   ◆   **Aries:** The Aries personality wants to control the money in the house and will be adamant about this. Every coin goes through their hands before it goes elsewhere. The best way for an Aries to make money is either by selling personal creations or ideas, or by vying for jobs that will eventually put you in a position of authority.

- **Taurus:** Taurus, although sometimes bull-headed about a budget, has a very pragmatic approach to finances. There will always be a sound budget in place, and a bit of bumper room for emergencies. The best way for people born under this sign to make money is through an artistic outlet or an artistically oriented job.

- **Gemini:** Gemini hates balancing their budget and really has no idea where those twenty-five dollars went last week. Typically, no one should trust Gemini to utilize credit cards or cash responsibly because they use both like water, not really thinking much about the bills to follow. Nonetheless, people born under this sign can make money from writing, teaching, or other challenging careers that keep them from getting bored quickly.

- **Cancer:** One of the finest signs for solid finances on every front. Cancers win at bets, are wise with stocks, and know how to handle every portion of a home's economics with a shrewd eye. The best place for Cancer to make money professionally is in a job that deals with the public, especially a public accounting firm or financial management company.

- **Leo:** Leos are great at working with financial changes. If something shifts suddenly, for boon or bane, you can depend on a Leo to find a way to work with that situation and come out shining. Professionally, Leos make the most money in highly visible jobs where they can be somewhat in the spotlight.

- **Virgo:** Virgo tends to be a bit impulsive with money, especially when it comes to philosophical investments. They feel that money spent on a good cause or for "brain food" is well spent, even if other things suffer a little. On the career front, Virgos quickly become prosperous and successful in jobs like detective work and politics.

- **Libra:** The Libra personality is not at all happy when finances start looking thin. This person wants security in black and white; no gray allowed. Consequently,

Libras don't enjoy having to confront people about loans (either asking for one or getting back monies owed). In business, Libras tend to fare well no matter the choice of profession, so long as they perceive the associated profession and business as staying on an even financial keel.

- **Scorpio:** Scorpio goes to extremes with money. Either they're spending every last dime and getting in debt or saving like crazy, with nothing in between. In other words, don't ask a Scorpio to balance the budget! The best way for a Scorpio to make money professionally is through highly skilled work.

- **Sagittarius:** Generally, Sagittarians are successful with money. Even when something goes awry, they seem to have a flexible nature that can recoup losses gracefully and put windfalls to work. People born under this sign can make money in sports professions or in any job that allows them to provide insights and advice, which they have in abundance.

- **Capricorn:** Capricorns are excellent budgeters with patience akin to a saint. You want someone to barter or haggle for you? Find a Capricorn and get the deal of a lifetime even after paying a professional fee! In business, Capricorns excel in trade negotiations or anything that requires strong methodology, such as science.

- **Aquarius:** You will rarely see an Aquarian remember to their track spending. Their approach to money will always be unconventional, such as betting on emerging stocks rather than something more stable. For money-making propositions, the Aquarian should look to the field of research and development or other cutting-edge businesses.

- **Pisces:** Pisceans like security, being the motherly sort to begin with. They will nurture funds as they would any proverbial child. Nonetheless, if the decision about how money gets spent becomes a tug of war between head and heart, heart will win every time. For work, Pisces should look to any career that stimulates the imagination, such as art and writing.

Although this is just a general list, it's a good starting point. Besides getting to know your astro-self better, you can use this list to seek out people with an aptitude you might be lacking for financial help! However, astrology doesn't stop there.

Get yourself a good astrological calendar (one that lists Moon signs, Moon phases, transits, and so on). Before making financial decisions or changes, and before working any magic for the same, consider what the Moon sign is and then determine your best course of action. The following will help get you started.

Money and Moon Signs

- ◆ **Moon in Aries:** Not a good time to make any financially risky move. While everything around you is rushing, you should probably wait and think things through thoroughly. Cast spells or work rituals for breaking down any barriers standing between you and success so that when this Moon sign passes, you can act with confidence.

- ◆ **Moon in Taurus:** Do not make any dramatic financial changes until this Moon sign has passed. Think, instead, of continuity and general maintenance. Work magic focused on your ability to follow through, which in turn leads to productivity and abundance.

- ◆ **Moon in Gemini:** Read over financial paperwork carefully, looking for fine print. Basically, the package you've been presented with may not be as good as you think. Also be aware that communications about money may be askew. Consider working spells that keep both your budget and your spirit in balance.

- **Moon in Cancer:** Don't let your heart lead your head with regard to a financial choice. No matter how much you might want to help what seems to be a good cause, remember the proverb that says that "the road to hell is paved with good intentions." Focus your magic on prosperity that comes from personal creativity.

- **Moon in Leo:** If a monetary opportunity comes your way, seize the day! The Moon in Leo is very money friendly. This is an excellent time to support your skills, knowledge, and prosperity goals with both mundane and spiritual efforts.

- **Moon in Virgo:** An excellent time to shop for deals and watch for unique opportunities. Also, don't be afraid to spend a little money on your mental development. An overall good sign for any type of money magic.

- **Moon in Libra:** If you're thinking about investing in art, this is the best time to go looking. You will find a treasure that either pays off immediately or that builds long-term equity. Spiritually, meditate on improving your discernment of how you use money and how it affects your life.

- **Moon in Scorpio:** If something looks too good to be true, it is! This is not a good time for making get-rich-quick deals or signing loan papers; for that matter, don't sign any paperwork if you can avoid it. Magically focus on protecting your resources and turning away any negative energy aimed at your direction.

- **Moon in Sagittarius:** Something out of the ordinary might come your way, and if this happens, look at it with avid interest and close scrutiny. This may be opportunity knocking! Just take care to be wholly honest in your deals and with your ability to follow through on those dealings. Spiritually speaking, this sign supports goal-oriented magic.

◆ **Moon in Capricorn:** Whatever personal ground rules you have for your budget and spending, stick to them wholly! Don't look for the easy way out financially; let your hard work speak for itself. In spellcraft and ritual, work on developing a strong sense of focus, tenacity, and follow-through.

◆ **Moon in Aquarius:** Social interaction may bring unexpected financial rewards during this sign. When this opportunity presents itself, however, don't wait too long to jump on it; it's short-lived, and delays will likely close that window firmly. In your sacred space, work magic that's aimed at refilling the well of inspiration for everything you do.

◆ **Moon in Pisces:** When you find yourself wavering on a financial matter, stop listening to everyone else and key into your inner voice. It will not lead you astray. In fact, as well-meaning as friends and family may be, they could be guiding you in the completely wrong direction! Magically speaking, this is a sign that represents the proverbial miracle. Wherever you need one financially is the area in which to direct your spells and rituals.

Chinese Astrology

Now, if that wasn't enough to start with, there's also Chinese astrology to consider! Based on very similar concepts as Western astrology, the Chinese zodiac has one cycle every twelve years. During each cycle, one of twelve animals rule for one year each.

The chart on the following page will help you determine under which animal sign you (or someone else) were born.

Patricia Telesco

Year of the Rat	Year of the Ox	Year of the Tiger	Year of the Cat
1948	1949	1950	1951
1960	1961	1962	1963
1972	1973	1974	1975
1984	1985	1986	1987
1996	1997	1998	1999
2008	2009	2010	2011
2020	2021	2022	2023

Year of the Dragon	Year of the Snake	Year of the Horse	Year of the Goat
1952	1953	1954	1955
1964	1965	1966	1967
1976	1977	1978	1979
1988	1989	1990	1991
2000	2001	2002	2003
2012	2013	2014	2015
2024	2025	2026	2027

Year of the Monkey	Year of the Rooster	Year of the Dog	Year of the Boar
1956	1957	1958	1959
1968	1969	1970	1971
1980	1981	1982	1983
1992	1993	1994	1995
2004	2005	2006	2007
2016	2017	2018	2019
2028	2029	2030	2031

Similar to Western astrology, each of the animal signs has personality traits that can help you better understand how you handle money matters. Again, these are generalizations that can be further improved by learning more about the Eastern system, including how the day and hour of your birth also has an animal sign that affects traits!

- **Rat:** Rats value financial security highly, making them akin to Virgos. People born in the Year of the Rat always want to know where every dime and nickel goes (with footnotes!). Although this detail is frustrating to people around the Rat, Rat finds it very beneficial because it nearly always keeps them in the black! Rats are great financial handlers and always know a good money-making deal when they see one. Professionally, Rats make amazing accountants or marketers and also excel in anything requiring detail, including writing.
- **Ox:** The Ox does nothing quickly when it comes to money. For this person, the method of reaching one's goal is everything. In fact, the method becomes important to the point where it becomes an almost unobtainable ideal rather than something that's getting done. This is why Ox rarely fares well with short-term investments. To profit at work, an Ox is best to look to jobs that do not require constant change and adaptation. Constancy is a key word for this sign.
- **Tiger:** Tigers are not the best people to trust with money. Like Geminis, they tend to be very reckless with it, wanting to jump into uninvestigated and risky opportunities. They also can be overly generous, especially if there's a good cause under paw! To succeed at business, Tigers should be in a semi-authoritarian role, with someone else more subdued and even-handed at the helm.
- **Cat:** Cats are very ambitious and tend to put their money toward those ambitions or toward play. Even when playing, however, Cats aren't foolhardy. They're always

working toward a steady progression forward. Even when that progress isn't obtainable, Cat knows how to stay on their feet in difficult financial situations. When wishing to make a prosperous career for themselves, Cats are best in working alone, telecommuting, or with only a few other people so their social drive doesn't get in the way of prosperity or success.

- **Dragon:** Dragons are smart, but not overly frugal. They want the best in life (what Dragon wouldn't?), which means living like a king even when the budget is one suited to a peasant! When discussing financial matters, don't expect a Dragon to be the least bit tactful. Whatever their idea is on the subject, it will be demanding and idealistic. As for jobs, Dragons reap the most rewards from working solo, much like Cats.

- **Snake:** For the most part, Snakes will be very lucky and wise with money. The only time this fortune and sagacity slips is when it comes to the way others perceive them. Snakes have a strong need to appeal to people. If it means spending a little extra to achieve that goal, it's spent! As for earning money, Snakes excel at any job that requires decision-making.

- **Horse:** Horses have financial aptitude of a very domestic nature. Even so, they hesitate to listen to even the best financial advice when it's offered. Additionally, God help Horse's budget when they have a mission; all else fades when focused on a goal. With this in mind, a Horse can find prosperity in jobs that require a lot of drive and headstrong fortitude.

- **Goat:** Goats avoid looking at their bank statements and budgets, which are probably stacked in a dusty corner somewhere. The only time these are pulled out is when Goat wants to gather money for something that purportedly improves life's quality. Sadly, the Goat's perception of an improvement isn't always a good one. Professionally, Goats should avoid work that requires stringent deadlines. Rather, they need something that allows them to work at their own pace, if possible, with the public.

- **Monkey:** The Monkey will always be creative with money and frequently a little mischievous with it! If there's a new toy on the market, the Monkey will want to buy it right away rather than waiting for the price to go down. Nonetheless, Monkeys excel in seeing opportunity when it avails itself, and therefore usually succeed. They do well at careers that let them play, such as comedy, theater or television.

- **Rooster:** Roosters should not handle money that's aimed at long-term goals. They know nothing of groundwork and will opt for fancy over functionality just so they can crow about something new. For a job, Roosters need to watch for openings that allow them to brag and swagger as loud and long as they wish; in other words, avoid being a diplomat!

- **Dog:** Dogs will worry and fuss over money no matter how good things may be. They are also very single-minded about how they should spend money and how to keep track of it. About the only time they waiver from this is when someone or something to whom they're loyal needs monetary help, and then the Dog is right at the heel of the situation. To succeed in business, Dogs do well in humanitarian jobs such as nursing, where their loyalty and sacrifice of personal time will shine. The only caution for Dog is to not give so much that they burn themself out.

- **Boar:** If there is an animal sign with the word *sucker* labeled on it, Boar would be at the top of the list. Boars are so sincere and dutiful that people take advantage of them on every level, including financially. Consequently, but for day-to-day affairs, Boars should let someone more shrewd handle large investments. For employment, the Boar makes an excellent researcher or scientist, sometimes to the point of genius, because they will not be easily dissuaded until they accomplish a goal.

As with the Moon signs discussed previously, each of the Chinese years has an influence on what's happening in a person's life and the overall energies of the universe. You can use your knowledge of this, combined with Moon signs, to determine the best way to apply funds, or what type of spell and rituals to hold. Following is a brief overview to get you started.

Animal Year Influences

- **Year of the Rat:** Oxen can save money this year; Tigers will reach an equilibrium (money comes in, then it goes right back out again). Cats will likely have a minor setback, Dragons should invest any extra they have, Snakes need to take care not to overextend their resources, and Horses should avoid any new business deals. Goats may experience serious monetary losses now, but Monkeys prosper no matter what they do! Roosters see opportunity but should be wary; this isn't what it seems. Dogs will experience a financially dull year, while Boars experience tremendous success.

- **Year of the Ox:** Rats need to be frugal now, and Ox continues to have a solid flow of income (all of which results from hard work). Tigers should avoid risky investments, Cats begin to recover from the year before, and Dragons may have a falling-out with their boss. Snake will have to work very hard this year to maintain any forward movement. Horses can anticipate good business, and Goats and Dogs will want to forget this year ever happened. Monkey and Rooster do well financially. Boars will have to be ready to make fast changes to keep prosperity flowing.

- **Year of the Tiger:** Rats and Oxen have a rather iffy year financially and should take care to not spend without good cause. Tiger's life improves. Cats have to cope with a lot of transformations to keep money coming in; Dragons are successfully accomplishing goals. Snake learns a lot but doesn't necessarily *earn* a lot. Horse receives some new opportunities with real financial possibilities attached, Goat maintains (barely), and Monkey is having fun! Rooster has a lousy year, and Dog and Boar seem to keep finances in a tenuous state of balance.

- **Year of the Cat:** Rats need to watch their proverbial tails this year, lest any financial nets be completely cut off. Oxen find their hooves are back on more solid ground. Tiger continues to thrive, as does Cat, who purrs happily with new toys in their own year. The Dragon's riches improve now, especially around the lair, as does the Dragon's smaller cousin, the Snake, but in a similarly smaller way. Horse has a great year in business, and even the Goat gets some long-overdue advancement. Monkey, again, has a great year in their career. Roosters and Dogs maintain uniform budgets. Finally, the Boar needs to be wary of legal matters that could tap finances.
- **Year of the Dragon:** Rat, Tigers, Snakes, and even Cats, who are forever wanting more, seem content with money this year. Ox has to establish some secure foundations before finances can improve. Dragons, of course, are having an amazing year, and Goats and Monkeys aren't far behind. Rooster turns their attention away from money toward nurturing relationships, and Boars have a reclusive time focusing on a few set, important ambitions.
- **Year of the Snake:** Rats should avoid business this year, if possible, especially something new. Ox needs to watch how money is being spent at home. Tiger wants to invest the money from better years in some travel or other type of adventure, and Cats and Dragons continue to fare quite nicely. If you're a Snake, try the impossible; it may just manifest. Horses spend a lot of time and money on a matter of the heart, but this may

be for naught. Goats will have an engaging financial year, and Monkeys find a new opportunity with which to play. How that opportunity fleshes out, though, isn't wholly certain. Roosters may discover a lot of little repair bills cropping up at home, Dogs get a chance to find a new focus for their efforts, and Boars have a generally sound business year.

◆ **Year of the Horse:** The Rat will discover more debts than even their clever mind can handle this year. The best bet, by far, is to cut their losses. Meanwhile, the Ox excels in their career. Tigers start something new to advance themselves, Cats continue to have a fairly good year, and Dragons (seeming to have all the luck) follow suit. The Snake may hold their ground with money matters but finds other parts of life unsatisfying at best; the poor Horse is wondering why this year was named after them! Goats and Monkeys often find better jobs, and Roosters see raises or promotions. Boars need to stay organized and on task to keep from experiencing losses.

◆ **Year of the Goat:** The Rat begins to get a handle on debts now, but the Oxen find themselves in the Rat's shoes from last year. Tigers should be wary; there's trouble on the horizon. Cats have a few setbacks, as do Dragons, though nothing devastating. Snakes can hold their own but not expect a lot of advancement. Horse and Goat have a steadily improving year. Monkey plans for a good year, but that's about all that happens: plans. Rooster gets themself in a jam that might require reconstruction, and Dog isn't doing much better. Boars, however, see a light at the end of the tunnel and enjoy some forward movement.

◆ **Year of the Monkey:** Ah, glorious relief for the Rat, who finds the bottom line balancing out and growing. The poor Ox is no better off than before. Tigers can experience gains from good ideas; Cats should carefully pace finances. Dragons are best off if they stay out of the limelight this year, and Snakes aren't doing much better, needing to learn to cope with less. Horses would do well financially in a political atmosphere, but Goats retreat to the quiet life, not earning tons but not spending a lot either. For the Monkey, this year is party city, and Roosters join in with plenty of pomp and pampering to crow about. Dogs should be careful not to get into sticky monetary situations, and the Boar has a very solid and enjoyable year.

- **Year of the Rooster:** Rats are happily back on the track to success. Ox finally gets a reprieve, but Tiger does not and is none too happy. Cats likewise meow with displeasure at the turn in personal investments, and even the Dragon has to be cautious this year. The Horse and Boar will both thrive in business. Goat can take some fruits from previous years and go on vacation! Monkey is no longer playful, being faced with growing monetary restrictions, Dogs are still licking their wounds from unsound decisions of the previous year, and the Rooster blusters with impressive success.

- **Year of the Dog:** Rats can have a good year if they keep their minds focused on business. Oxen and Goats won't enjoy this year much and will feel the weight of unexpected and often unusually high expenses. Tigers spend money on good causes, and Cats are very cautious and hesitant to invest (with good reason). Dragons will take over financially again, Snakes do okay but aren't working very hard on making improvements, and the dependable Horse works for both sound income and personal fulfillment. Poor Monkey is still not playing, because they have to use all that energy just to keep afloat. Finally, Dogs do very well now, being rewarded for steadfastness, and Boars achieve a steady income.

- **The Year of the Boar:** Rats should plan money carefully and begin saving for the future. The Ox gets a welcome reprieve, and Tigers have more good luck than they know what to do with. Cat is quite content and secure now, Dragon gets a financial boon from investments, and Snake simply sits in the grass waiting for the year to end. Horses have money and finally can spend some of it on themselves. Goats, Boars, and Monkeys will all be seeing unexpected profits. Roosters have to keep their beaks to the grindstone to keep the bills paid, and the Dog returns to a quieter existence, being careful to guard the resources on hand.

Feng Shui

Feng shui, or the art of placement, has existed in various forms for at least 3,500 years, and originated in China. By its very design, feng shui works with an environment's energy (called *chi*) and gently shifts that energy toward specific goals and overall improvements for the body, mind, and spirit of everyone and everything in that environment. As a person or whole family, learns how to work with chi (instead of against it), the result is a greater abundance of happiness, well-being, and, yes, even money!

To use feng shui to help with money matters, first you have to understand the basics of this philosophical system. Feng shui breaks out every area (be it a whole building, a house, or a room) by its directional points. Within each directional point lies a specific type of energy that can help you understand more about yourself, your present situation(s), and the way you handle money. Better still, effective use of this energy can help you improve any problematic area, not just those dealing with finances.

Following is a brief overview and some ideas to get you started.

Feng Shui Regions and Energies

- **North:** The northern part of your home or workplace nurtures finances, assists in job-seeking, wrangles head-on with office politics, affects the way others perceive your work (putting it in a better light), and is helpful with career-oriented magic. Make sure there is a touch of black or blue in this region to support the energy flow, along with something gold-toned (perhaps a flowering plant with a gold-colored pot).

    If the northern part of your home is a bathroom, you might find your career isn't doing well, or that you've chosen a job as a plumber! If the northern part of your home is a den, you may find that a career in research, counseling, or something else social is the key to prosperity. In any case, this is one of the best areas in which to work on your finances.

- **Northeast:** The northeast region empowers your ability to learn new skills for a job, or better apply and augment those you already have. Akin to the Eastern quarter in magic, a lot of conscious focus comes from the chi here. When you need your mind and eyes to be sharp, work magic in this area and decorate it with yellows or browns.

    If the northeast part of your home is a bedroom, you'll be tempted to study for your job in this space; this may or may not work for you. If the northeast part of your home is the kitchen, you probably find yourself hungry every time you apply your skills. No matter what, this is one of the best spots to choose for meditating on the next steps to take on the path to prosperity.

- **East:** The eastern region is supportive of new financial endeavors and creative money applications. For example, if you're trying to come up with a new marketing gimmick, cast your spell and do your groundwork here. East is also the best space to stimulate yourself, a situation, or another person toward steady improvements with money-or anything else, for that matter. The accent colors for this region are pale blue and shoot green.

When a money-making proposition is buried in red tape or taking way too much time, check this part of your work and living space. Clean up any clutter and remove barriers so the energy flows freely. By the way, if the eastern part of your home is a doorway, you may find opportunity knocking quite a bit. Just take care that not all openings are right for you, nor will all be fruitful.

◆ **Southeast:** This is the area from which your prosperity, and that of all members of your household flows, so tend it with care. When you need to improve overall abundance, make sure there are highlights of dark blue and green in this region, as well as something wooden (perhaps a change bank for symbolic value).

If you want your money to grow, keep a healthy plant in this part of your home or office (or both!). If you find that your ability to create new financial opportunities seems sluggish, spend a lot of time in this region considering your options. If this part of the home is unkempt, you may make some gains that have "shady" overtones. Any house that has a home office in this region is likely to see reasonable success.

◆ **South:** For money to come from personal renown or the recognition of your abilities and efforts, work within this part of your sacred space or home regularly. Just remember that fame and fortune can burn like the fires from the south, destroying or creating in the process of manifestation. Decorate this region with reds and purples for the best results.

If you're finding it hard to raise the zeal with which to empower your dreams, or that people don't seem to recognize your diligent efforts, check this area closely. Get rid of any clutter and open it up to as much natural light as possible.

- **Southwest:** The prosperity in this section comes from your relationships: having a successful mate, a helpful friend, or a wealthy family member, for example. It is also the best spot to work spells and rituals for personal luck, peace, de-stressing, and contentment (no matter the situation). To help keep this energy moving, highlight this region with browns and yellows.

    When you have trouble adjusting to financial changes, specifically those that affect your family harmony, review this space and give it loving attention. Make sure things aren't blocky; stress curves (no sharp angles) for greatest effect.

- **West:** When the children in and around your life need financial help, this is the area in which to be working your magic. Bring white, silver, or gold items into this space to accentuate its energies. Note that the results from this working will be aimed at helping the children help themselves versus raising more personal funds to support them.

    By the way, this area can relate to figurative children too, such as a writer's book, an artist's painting, and a social worker's successful charity!

- **Northwest:** This is the charity and service-oriented part of a home. In other words, you get from giving. Work magic for other people here, especially spells and rituals from which you will get no reward but the satisfaction of knowing you're doing something nice.

Additionally, you can enact spiritual processes here when you need financial help from others. When you do, the chi's giving nature moves out of this space to open hearts and pocketbooks, even those of stern financial managers and loan officers! It also helps you overcome the natural discomfort or embarrassment many people feel when asking for assistance.

Feng Shui Color Chart

Feng shui integrates color into its processes to help move energy in the direction desired. To use this additional dimension, you can light an appropriately colored candle in the segment of the house that best represents your financial goals, bring in a bouquet of flowers, or add other small color accents in that area for as long as necessary. Here is an overview of color associations.

- **Black:** Clarity about your money and how it should be used. Finding sound ways to stay "in the black."
- **Blue:** Creative applications for money that will result in happiness and wealth; double the effect by using this in the northern quarter of your home.
- **Gold:** A very wealthy color that, when combined with the southern quarter of the home, will encourage good health, too.
- **Green:** Add this into your wardrobe and your home when you need to improve business prospects, before making important business decisions, or when applying yourself tenaciously to a work-related situation.
- **Indigo:** Use this color to get the truth about a suspicious financial deal. It also helps you plan ahead for various projects that require a strong financial base. Most effective when combined with the northeast quarter.
- **Orange:** Improved awareness of the best possible timing for financial matters. Using money wisely; being dependable about financial obligations. Add to the southwest quarter to increase this color's power.
- **Purple:** Use this to loosen the purse strings a little, or when you need to take a leadership role in a financially oriented situation. Good overall color for abundance, especially when combined with the northwest quarter.

- **Red:** An excellent color for making shrewd financial moves, especially quick ones, which result in long-term happiness and security. Combine this with the southern quarter of the home.
- **Pink:** When you have to communicate about money in a tactful, gentle, and honest manner, pink is a great helpmate. Combine this with the southern quarter for improved impact.
- **Yellow:** For situations that require a mature, responsible outlook with regard to your budget or other financial matters, turn to yellow. This color improves mental keenness when focusing on those situations and your ability to communicate effectively about money. It may also be combined with general wish magic to speed manifestation. Most powerful in the southwest quarter of the living space.
- **White:** When something stands between you and financial success, choose white to break down those barriers. This can also help you make money from travel, protect what you already have, and break old cycles. Best combined with the western quarter.

Elementary, My Dear

Beyond using quarters and colors to improve the flow of chi, feng shui advocates adding specific elements into the living space. For example, the east and southeast center of your home is considered the wood element. If this area happens to be filled with metal, you might find that you spend a lot of unnecessary money on technological items. Replace some of the metal with wooden items to bring the room back into balance along with your budget. If you can't add actual wood to this space, use green-colored items instead.

Too much wood can lead you to feel very torn between your goals and dreams and concrete reality, especially in how you apply your paycheck. Money will likely come and go very quickly in this kind of environment. Balance out wood with a little Earth for foundations or some metal to provide a logical symmetry.

Here is a list of the four elements and their effects in feng shui:

- **Fire:** Fire is the element for the southern part of the living space. If this part of your home is dark all the time, you will never make money by being recognized for your talents. Open up the space to natural light, however, and a raise or promotion could soon be forthcoming! If you don't have a way of improving the natural light in this area of your home, add accent items colored red or purple or perhaps an ever-burning candle.

  If this part of your home is overly bright, you might find yourself burning out in your chosen career, that you're overly temperamental at the office, or that your money seems to disappear as if you'd simply tossed it on a fire. In this case, you want to decrease the amount of Fire in the southern part of your space or bring a little Water into the equation.

- **Water:** Water sits in the northern quarter of a room or home, and it's one of the best elements for your career. When things are lagging, get yourself a fountain or fish tank and place it near this region. Another office-oriented option would be a water cooler! Alternatively, add accents of blue and black.

  When there's too much of the Water element in the north, your career path may become unclear. You may also discover you lack a strong backbone in an office environment. Balance out the Water by adding some wood or Fire to those areas.

- **Metal:** The next element is metal, and it resides in the west and northwest. When you need to decrease lost time at work due to sickness or get reliable assistance on a pressing financial matter, add more metal into those parts of your office or home. The colors for metal are white, silver, and gold.

When there's too much metal in the north, you'll often find you're spending way too much on any metallic items (toasters, cars, and so on) or that you're overly focused on the material world. Too much metal in the west means your children will be costing you a lot of money. Earth and Water both help balance out too much metal in one's proverbial energy diet.

- **Earth:** The Earth element governs the southwest and northeast areas. When your chosen career seems to be constantly in a state of flux, when you find depression affecting your performance, or when you find you're having trouble applying yourself successfully to a new task, this element is lacking. Try adding a potted plant or the colors of brown, yellow, and tan to these regions to resolve the problem.

  When there's too much Earth in your environment, you'll tend to study your finances way too much, to the point of overlooking the obvious. You may also have a hard time switching gears from the mundane when trying to relate to spiritual matters. Balance Earth with wood or a bit of Fire.

Neutrality and Redirection

The one part of a room or home that we haven't talked about yet is the center. This is typically considered a wholly neutral zone in feng shui. It is an excellent area in which to work on remaining similarly neutral about difficult financial decisions or situations. If you can set up your magical money altar in this region, it also accents that sense of out-of-space, out-of-time and provides a nice mingling point for energies.

What happens when the area of your home, office, or room is (for whatever reason) inaccessible or unchangeable? Most of us move into a prefabricated home; that is, we don't have one custom designed specifically to improve the flow of chi. This means we have to work with what we're given. If the money center of our home is the bedroom, it's likely that you find yourself often sleepy at work, or when you're trying to focus on any monetary problem.

Similarly, if the money center is the toilet, you can guess what the cash flow is like!

Feng shui responds to these kinds of problems by using mirrors to redirect energy. You can hang a mirror so that it reflects energy away from an area or draws specific vibrations into it. The additional benefit here is that the mirror can also direct light, which helps keep your financial matters clear and focused. In the two previous examples, hanging a mirror above the toilet or adjacent to the bed should improve things.

Results Count

People often ask me about the results that can be achieved with feng shui. If you're looking for a lot of bells and whistles, this isn't the best system for you. Feng shui has a very gentle motion. It's not meant for dramatic transformation, but rather slow, steady change that works with nature and the space you have.

Additionally, feng shui stresses that a person must change as much as their environment to experience any degree of success. You must be ready to activate your mind, body, and spirit for abundant living, and be equally ready to accept that new life when it arrives. The gradual alterations that feng shui makes externally give you the opportunity to prepare yourself internally for the results. Indeed, this is the perfect balance of the phrase "as within, so without" on a very personal level, a level that will lead you toward prosperity.

Appendix 1

PROSPERITY COMPONENTS

Those readers wishing to have a ready reference for suitable offerings, libations, incense, and spell and ritual components for money magic will find information shared here very helpful. Here you can review various potential ingredients for their elemental associations, common magical applications, and deities to whom they were considered sacred. From there, it isn't too hard to design some magic suited to your needs, the ritual's focus, and/or the Sacred Power upon whom you may be calling for aid.

In reviewing this list, bear in mind it is very abbreviated and limited to commonly available stones, crystals, and edible items, because I know a lot of budget-minded Kitchen Witches out there. Nonetheless, everything in this world has potential for magic. If you're looking for more information on money magic components, I suggest books such as Paul Beyerl's *A Compendium of Herbal Magic;* *Cunningham's Encyclopedia of Crystal, Gem & Metal Magic* by Scott Cunningham; and my *Magic Made Easy: Charms, Spells, Potions, & Power.* All of these are great references to which you can turn again and again in your mystical arts.

Herbs, Spices, and Edibles

- **Allspice:** Fire. An herb of luck with money, overall prosperity, health (so you don't lose money to sick days), and productive number-crunching.
- **Almond:** Air. Very attuned to money matters (especially those that affect relationships) and improving self-sufficiency. Sacred to Artemis, Cybele, Hecate, and Zeus in Greece; Ptah in Egypt; and Chandra in India.
- **Anise:** Air. Use this when you need a little good energy or to encourage blessings from Apollo, Mercury, and Hermes (Greco-Roman).
- **Apple:** Water. Insight and prudence with your resources. Sacred to numerous deities, including Induna and Odin (Norse), Venus and Apollo (Roman), and Zeus and Hera (Greek).
- **Basil:** Fire. Use this to face difficult financial situations bravely. Sacred to Krishna and Vishnu (India).
- **Bay:** Fire. An herb that promotes success. Sacred to Eros, Apollo, and Adonis (Greece), Buddha (India), and Fides (Rome).
- **Caraway:** Air. If you're involved in an Earth-oriented profession, use caraway to improve your job performance and help use your resources wisely.
- **Carrot:** Fire. Carrots improve our vision, both spiritually and temporally. Use this when you need to look at your finances with a clear eye.
- **Catnip:** Water. When you need good instincts to guide you in a monetary decision or a little extra charm to improve your chances of getting a new line of credit, use catnip. Sacred to Bast (Egypt).
- **Celery:** Fire. Magically used for mental clarity; maybe nibble on some while you're balancing your budget!

- **Chamomile:** Fire. Use chamomile to augment your conscious, logical mind. Also, use it to bless a new project.
- **Cherry:** Water. Creativity and sensitivity with money matters. Sacred to the Maiden aspect of the Goddess.
- **Cinnamon:** Fire. A good aromatic for personal fortitude and overall success.
- **Clove:** Fire. An herb for protecting your prosperity and love. If you have a Malaysian god or goddess that you follow, this is considered a suitable offering for them.
- **Coconut:** Water. Excellent for intuitive use of money or any other lunar attribute you may need.
- **Coffee:** Fire. Stimulates the conscious mind and improves alertness.
- **Currant:** Fire and Water. As with many berries, this fruit symbolizes Earth's abundance.
- **Daisy:** Water. Use this when you need to simplify a financial matter. Sacred to Freya (Germany).
- **Dandelion:** Air. A flower attuned to wishes as well as divinatory questions regarding your finances. Sacred to Hecate and Theseus (Greece).
- **Dill:** Fire. This herb protects your resources from those who would try to get them through deception.
- **Fennel:** Fire. Suited to banishing ill-intended magic that may be zapping your prosperity. Sacred to Prometheus (Greek).
- **Fig:** Fire. A fruit of profuseness. It also promotes your ability to use what you get with wisdom. Sacred to Ra and Isis (Egypt), Brahma (India), and Juno (Greece).
- **Garlic:** Fire. Use garlic for protecting that which you value and when working with the goddess Hecate (Greek).
- **Ginger:** Fire. An herb of victory, power, and prosperity.
- **Grain:** Earth. Providence and good fortune. Barley was sacred to Demeter (Greece) and Vishnu (India).

- **Grape:** Water. The fruit of abundance that encourages a reason for celebration. Sacred to Bacchus (Rome), Hathor (Egypt), and Izanagi (Japan).
- **Heather:** Water. Good fortune is found in this flower, especially for networking about financial matters. Used to invoke Isis (Egypt) and Venus (Rome).
- **Honey:** Air. Honey purifies, attracts happiness, motivates bounty, inspires romance, and generally brings "sweetness" to life. Sacred to many deities, including Min (Egypt), Ea (Babylon), Artemis (Greece), and Kama (India).
- **Kiwi:** Water. A fruit that improves hope.
- **Lavender:** Air. This herb deters the anxiety and stress that go with trying financial times. Sacred to Saturn (Rome).
- **Lemon:** Water. Lemon bears the energy of purification, which is great when you need a totally fresh start that ends with long-lasting results. Sacred to the Buddhist deity Jamb Hala.
- **Lime:** Water. Use lime juice to attract the Earth Fairy folk and devas, who can be helpful in building firm foundations.
- **Marigold:** Fire. Use this to discern the truth in any money matter. Sacred to Mary in Christianity.
- **Marjoram:** Air. An herb of bounty. Sacred to Venus (Rome) and therefore quite suited to marriage rituals.
- **Milk:** Water. Use this to nurture your investments. Sacred to Hathor and Isis (Egypt), and Zeus (Greek), among others.
- **Mint:** Air. An herb of success and prosperity. Mint can also grant some new life to a financial project that's grown cold. Sacred to Pluto (Rome).
- **Mulberry:** Air. This fruit grants wisdom, practicality, and inventiveness with one's finances. Sacred to Minerva (Rome).
- **Nutmeg:** Fire. Nutmeg brings overall good fortune. Sacred to many Indian gods and goddesses.

- **Orange:** Fire. Orange provides us with luck and prosperity. Sacred to Apollo and Hera (Greece).
- **Peach:** Water. Peaches bear the energy of longevity to any financial project. They also invoke wisdom in your dealings. Sacred to Hai Wang Ma (China) and Izanagi (Shinto).
- **Pineapple:** Fire. This promotes good fortune, especially in your dealings with other people, including when trying to get a loan.
- **Plum:** Water. Plums provide respect for your efforts. Used in offerings to Japanese gods and goddesses.
- **Pomegranate:** Fire. This fruit manifests creative application of money and overall prosperity. Sacred to Dionysus and Persephone (Greece), and Ceres (Rome), among others.
- **Raspberry:** Water. Use this to encourage abundance or to shake off negative influences.
- **Rose:** Water. A nice addition to divinatory work or spells to improve your intuition. Sacred to Venus (Rome) and Aphrodite (Greece).
- **Rosemary:** Fire. Promotes memory retention (so you know where that twenty dollars went!) and the responsible use of money. Sacred to Venus (Rome) and Mary (for Christianity).
- **Saffron:** Fire. Excellent herb for prosperity, as well as for fostering leadership skills when it comes to your household budget. Sacred to Eos (Greece) and Amon Ra (Egypt) and Brahma (Hindu).
- **Sage:** Air. Use this herb when you need to make sound financial decisions or promote good business sense. Sacred to Cronus (Rome) and Zeus (Greece).
- **Sugar:** Earth. A key ingredient to improve sour dispositions. Also, a good offering for ancestral spirits.

- **Thyme:** Water. Use thyme to motivate fortitude and financial awareness. A suitable offering for Fairies and devas.
- **Vanilla:** Water. Vanilla bean or pure flavoring is magically geared toward productivity.

Stones, Metals, and Minerals

- **Amethyst:** Water. Carry this when you're working on self-control with regard to your money. Sacred to Bacchus, Dionysus, and Diana (Roman). A good antitheft amulet.
- **Aventurine:** Air. Increases perception, especially when working with iffy financial decisions and situations. A good gambling talisman.
- **Bloodstone:** Fire. Use this when you're facing legal fees or legal situations that could be costly to insure your victory. Carried in your wallet or purse, this also attracts money.
- **Brass:** Fire. A substitute for gold, this is an overall money metal, but it is not as strong as gold.
- **Carnelian:** Fire. Use this to effectively communicate about financial problems or situations.
- **Cat's-Eye:** Earth. A gambler's talisman that protects what you have and encourages prosperity. Good when you're working investment magic.
- **Chrysoprase:** Earth. A success stone. Sacred to Vesta (Rome).
- **Coal:** Earth. An overall money stone.
- **Copper:** Water. Use this to improve your luck with money. Sacred to Aphrodite (Greek), Astarte (Canaanite), and Ishtar (Assyro-Babylonian).
- **Coral:** Water. Use when you need to use your resources wisely. Also, a good antitheft charm. Sacred to Isis (Egypt) and Venus (Rome).
- **Fluorite:** Air. Improves knowledge skills and mental focus for your career.

- **Hematite:** Fire. Use for establishing strong foundations. An alternative stone is obsidian.
- **Iron:** Fire. This will help you recover any stolen or lost goods. Sacred to Selene (Greece).
- **Jade:** Water. A money-attracting stone that also helps heal difficult financial situations. Sacred to Kwan Yin (China), Maat (Egypt), and Buddha (Tibet).
- **Lodestone:** Water. Use this to "attract" prosperity.
- **Malachite:** Earth. Emphasizes business success.
- **Quartz:** Fire. An overall energy-boosting stone. The green form of quartz is particularly good for money magic.
- **Rhodonite:** Fire. Promotes mental clarity.
- **Salt:** Earth. Establishing firm foundations, protecting your resources, and improving financial flow. Sacred to Aphrodite (Greece).
- **Silver:** Water. Although the modern value of silver has lessened, it has a similar prosperous energy to gold, only to a lesser degree. Sacred to Isis (Egypt), Luna (Rome), Selene (Greek), and many other lunar goddesses.
- **Tiger eye:** Fire. Luck with money, improved divinatory efforts with regard to financial questions, and protection.
- **Tourmaline:** Water. Green is particularly useful for luck in business, pink opens the path for a positive reception at the loan office, and black helps banish negative financial situations.

Appendix II

GODS AND GODDESSES OF PROSPERITY AND PLENTY

For readers who would like to call on a specific aspect of the Divine to guide and bless their money magic efforts, these global gods and goddesses are provided with place of origin, brief description, and the specific dominions over which they have control. Remember that you should always establish a sound relationship with a god or goddess before asking such powers for favors. That's akin to going to a stranger's door and saying "gimme," and it will be greeted with similar affront.

- **Abundia (Rome):** Goddess who embodies the Earth's abundance. Honor her with living plants.
- **Adibuddha (Hindu):** The ultimate male essence. Call on this god when you need to get to the point of a financial matter instead of battling red tape. Honor him with lotus.
- **Aditi (Hindu):** Mother goddess who presides over protection and guidance in any situation. Honor her by working on Sunday.

- **Aeons (Gnostic):** Goddesses of thought, especially thought that manifests in concrete action. Honor them by using the number eight or twenty-two in your spell or ritual somehow.
- **Agassou (Benin/Haitian):** This guardian god can guide you to finding the best path to prosperity. Honor him with spring water.
- **Ahsonnutli (Navajo):** Hermaphroditic deity and creator, this god teaches balance, including with your budget!
- **Ahura Mazda (Persian):** Lord of knowledge who can guide you in learning new skills or honing those you already have. Honor him with kind acts and feathers.
- **Aje Saluga (Yoruban):** God of good fortune and wealth. Honor him with a cowrie shell.
- **Aker (Egypt):** This god watches over the meeting point of the East and West, granting his followers a unique perspective. Honor him with lion images or gold hues.
- **Amon Ra (Egypt):** God of the Sun who shines a light on any confusing situation and blesses us with abundance. Honor him with turquoise, olive oil, or cedar incense.
- **Ana (Ireland):** Goddess of prosperity and abundance.
- **Anagke (Greek):** Goddess of necessity and destiny who will help keep your finances on an even keel.
- **Ano (Assyro-Babylonian):** God of destiny on whom you may call to wish for overall improvements. Honor him with any woven item or star motifs.
- **Apollo (Greece/Rome):** God who can help you use money creatively or who can help you make money from an art. Additionally, he is a good god to call on for eloquence when communicating about finances. Honor him with bay leaves, sunflower, cinnamon, or orchids.
- **Athena (Greek):** Goddess whose blessing improves intelligence and provides a sense of inner peace about the bottom line. Honor her with flute music or geraniums.

- **Attis (Anatolian):** A resurrected god who restores. Honor him with snowdrops, lamps, and bread.
- **Aya (Assyro-Babylonian):** Goddess of law, order, and justice on whom you may call for legal assistance. Honor her with solar imagery.
- **Baduh (Semitic):** God of messages who can share your needs with the universe and open the way for understanding from others. Invoke him by writing the numbers eight, six, four, or two.
- **Baldur (Scandinavian):** Sun god who offers wisdom.
- **Befana (Italy):** Gift-bearing goddess who may provide an unexpected windfall. Honor her by sweeping the sacred space with a broom.
- **Benten (Japan):** Goddess of both luck and money, she is the patron of game players. Honor her with dragon images, swords, or ships.
- **Bishamon (Japan):** God of wealth and happiness. Honor him by working in the northern quarter of the sacred space.
- **Blodeuwedd (Welsh):** Goddess who can help you break a negative financial cycle or outmoded ideas about handling money. Honor her with owl imagery.
- **Bona Dea (Rome):** The good goddess who embodies prosperity and abundance. Honor her with vines or wine.
- **Brigid (Irish):** Goddess of fertility (both figurative and literal) who can inspire answers to your needs. Honor her with lit candles, images of arrows, or by working on February 1.
- **Buddhi (Tibetan):** Goddess of intelligence and intuition who can help you balance head and heart with regard to money matters. Honor her with elephant imagery.
- **Cerridwen (Welsh):** Goddess of inspiration and knowledge. Honor her with cauldrons or corn.
- **Damballa (Haiti):** Father of wisdom and reassurance. Honor him with living plants.
- **Dua (Egypt):** The personification of today who reminds us live presently and attentively.

- **Ernutet (Egypt):** Goddess of plenty.
- **Fa (Benin):** God of destiny who can help transform future financial matters.
- **Fulla (Norse):** Goddess of abundance.
- **Ganesh (India):** God of removing obstacles, wealth, and luck. Honor him with elephant images.
- **Hanuman (Hindu):** God of learning and education. Honor him with sandalwood incense.
- **Hatif (Arabic):** The spirit of good advice on whom you can call to be guided to the best person to help you with a money problem. Honor him with an oil lamp.
- **Iris (Greek):** Goddess of the rainbow who will take a message of your monetary need from Earth to heaven. Honor her with honied breads.
- **Isara (Mesopotamian):** Goddess of oaths and of good judgment on whom you can call when you're making a financial commitment. Honor her with snake imagery.
- **Janus (Roman):** God of doorways, on whom you can call to open the path to prosperity. Honor him with musk incense.
- **Kaukas (Lithuanian):** Guardian spirit of treasure and luck on whom you can call when you need good financial fortune or a windfall. Honor this spirit with dragon images.
- **Kwan Yin (China):** Goddess of mercy and generosity. Honor her with gold necklaces, dragon images, or willow.
- **Kuvera (Tibetan):** God of wealth and treasures. Honor him in the northern quarter of your sacred space.
- **Lakshmi (India):** Goddess who embodies all forms of wealth. Honor her with lotus, pearls, or gold-toned items.
- **Ma'at (Egypt):** Goddess of justice, truth, law, and order who you can call on for legal assistance or to help bring organization to your finances. Honor her with a red feather.
- **Metis (Greek):** Goddess of wisdom and good advice. Honor her with pregnant goddess images.

- **Mithra (Persia):** God of victory. Honor him by wearing yellow or gold items.
- **Morpheus (Greek):** God of dreams on whom you can call for a helpful night vision.
- **Nabu (Assyro-Babylonian):** God of scribes and wisdom on whom you might call when balancing the budget.
- **Nahmauit (Egyptian):** Goddess who removes negativity. Honor her with images of a sistrum.
- **Ninkarrak (Chaldean):** Goddess of healing who also banishes bad luck, on whom you can call to "heal" a streak of financial woes.
- **Njord (Scandinavian):** God of riches and prosperity. Honor him with sea water or sea salt.
- **Odin (Scandinavian):** God of cunning on who you can call when you need to be very clever with your funds. Honor him with rainwater.
- **Ops (Greek):** Goddess whose name gave birth to the word *opulence*. Honor her with harvest items or by working on her festival days of August 25 and September 19.
- **Oshrun (West Indian):** Goddess of gold and money. Honor her with a pumpkin.
- **Pingala (Hindu):** Goddess who embodies a cosmic force for manifestation on whom you can call when you need your money magic to manifest more quickly. Honor her with twelve-point motifs.
- **Pukkeenegak (Eskimo):** Goddess of providence on whom you can call when you need to stretch your resources further. Honor her with body paints.
- **Quetzalcoatl (Aztec):** God of practical knowledge who will help you apply your money wisely. Honor him with feathers.
- **Sanjna (Hindu):** Goddess of agreement on whom you might call to get a positive response on a loan or credit request. Honor her with three-pointed motifs or horse imagery.

- **Shing-mu (China):** Goddess of perfected intelligence who can help your mental focus and awareness when working on a difficult financial matter. Honor her with books or other symbols of learning.
- **Sin (Chaldean):** God of time who reminds us that time is, indeed, money. Honor him with silver items or lapis.
- **Spes (Rome):** Goddess of hope. Honor her with flowers and grains.
- **Sphynx (Egypt and Greece):** Guardians of treasures who may help you uncover a treasure of your own. Honor them with a riddle.
- **Terminus (Rome):** Fixer of boundaries who can help you establish financial boundaries too. Honor him with simple stones.
- **Themis (Greek):** Goddess of balance and good advice. Honor her with an offering of any elixir.
- **Wepwwer (Egyptian):** Opener of the way on whom you can call to create opportunities. Honor him with yellow items.
- **Yachimato-Hime (Japan):** Goddess of many roads on whom you can call when you need an alternative path to reach your financial goals.

Bibliography

Aldington, Richard, translator. New Larousse *Encyclopedia of Mythology*. Hamlyn Publishing, 1973.

Ann, Martha and Dorothy Myers Imel. *Goddesses in World Mythology*. Oxford University Press, 1995.

Beyerl, Paul. *Herbal Magic*. Phoenix Publishing, 1998.

Bruce-Mitford, Miranda. Illustrated *Book of Signs and Symbols*. DK Publishing, 1996.

Budge, E. A. Wallis. *Amulets and Superstitions*. Oxford University Press, 1930.

Cavendish, Richard. *A History of Magic*. Taplinger Publishing, 1979.

Cooper, J. C. *Symbolic and Mythological Animals*. Aquarian Press, 1992.

Cunningham, Scott. *Crystal, Gem, and Metal Magic*. Llewellyn Publications, 1995.

—. *Encyclopedia of Magical Herbs*. Llewellyn Publications, 1988.

—. *Magic in Food*. Llewellyn Publications, 1991.

Davison, Michael Worth, editor. *Everyday Life Through the Ages*. Reader's Digest Association Ltd., 1992.

Gordon, Leslie. *Green Magic*. Viking Press, 1977.

Gordon, Stuart. *Encyclopedia of Myths and Legends*. Headline Book Publishing, 1993.

Hall, Manly P. *Secret Teachings of All Ages*. Philosophical Research Society, 1977.

Jordan, Michael. *Encyclopedia of Gods*. Facts on File, Inc., 1993.

Kunz, George Frederick. *Curious Lore of Precious Stones*. Dover Publications, 1971.

Leach, Maria, editor. *Standard Dictionary of Folklore, Mythology, and Legend.* Harper & Row, 1984.

Leach, Marjorie. *Guide to the Gods.* ABC-Clio, 1992.

Lurker, Manfred. *Dictionary of Gods and Goddesses, Devils and Demons.* Routledge & Kegan Paul Ltd., 1995.

Miller, Gastavus Hindman. *Ten Thousand Dreams Interpreted.* M. A. Donohuse & Co., 1931.

Telesco, Patricia. *Folkways.* Llewellyn Publications, 1995.

—. *Futuretelling.* Crossing Press, 1997.

—. *Herbal Arts.* Crossed Crow Books, 2024.

—. *Kitchen Witch's Cookbook.* Llewellyn Publications, 1994.

—. *Magic Made Easy: Charms, Spells, Potions, & Power.* HarperOne, 1999.

—. *The Language of Dreams.* Crossing Press, 1997.

Walker, Barbara. *The Woman's Dictionary of Symbols and Sacred Objects.* Harper & Row, 1988.

Waring, Philippa. *The Dictionary of Omens and Superstitions.* Chartwell Books, 1978.

Wasserman, James. *Art and Symbols of the Occult* Destiny Books, 1993.